Praise for Gian Kumar's Books

Having found inner peace, he (the author) reinforces his belief that knowledge is the greatest to mankind as he imparts his experiential learning in an attempt to inspire others to find meaning in their lives as well.

– Free Press Journal

This book is written after a wide research on the subject and hence its validity cannot be doubted. What is good about this book is that it does not give any moral lessons. It just tells you in a rational way about your infinite potential to find your ultimate state of bliss and peace.

This book encourages people to go beyond the realm of peace into the realm of science. We human associate ourselves with our thoughts. Thus I come into existence. It restricts us from connecting with the world. Our consciousness lies beyond our ego. It creates a sense of oneness with all. It does not look at itself as a separate entity. It looks at itself in union with the universe. Hence the author suggests some paths of yoga to reach this stage. This has been also suggested by other authors in their books on spirituality.

– Afternoon Voice

In the first of his series of 3 books -Know Thyself, Think from The Heart and The Ultimate Reality, Gian Kumar answers some of the most pressing spiritual questions

– DNA

As you peruse the extensive elaborations of the self herein, regarding knowledge, awareness and realization, you will surely find the help needed in transforming your life to reach the fullness and completion you yearn for and deserve. The Gian Kumar explains it all - The truer self lies within. it needs courage to be coaxed out, accepted and loved. "I could do it," he says and raises a question: Can you?

– Mumbai Messenger

Gian Kumar answers our questions related to spirituality in a simple and seamless manner. The core of this series is based upon the absolute reality of life-oneness between the self and the universe.

– The Asian Age

So you feel you truly know yourself? Well, you can get hold of the book - Know Thyself and have an insightful journey to discover your true self. It is an amalgamation of the author's knowledge and thoughts in science, spirituality and philosophy. A worth read!

– Planet Powai

From time immemorial, people have searched for definitive responses to questions such as: Who am I, where do I come from and does God exist? What is the essence of my relationship with him? Know Thyself by Gian Kumar attempts to answer such philosophical questions in a reader-friendly format.

– Society Magazine

Know Thyself is a book by inquisitive thinker. Born in Burma to a religious Hindu family and raised by traditional principles Gian Kumar is a deep, inquisitive thinker who moved towards spirituality after struggling with his curiosity regarding God and his purpose of existence. Spirituality provided him with a framework or morality and helped him become a better person.

– Trinity Mirror

Think from the Heart Love from the Mind

BOOK II

Gian Kumar

ISBN 978-93-52013-73-9
© Gian Kumar, 2015
Cover: Deepanshu Rishi
Layouts: Ajay Shah
Printing: Thomson Press (India) Limited.

Published in India 2015 by
CELESTIAL BOOKS
An imprint of
LEADSTART PUBLISHING PVT LTD
Trade Centre, Level 1, Bandra Kurla Complex
Bandra (E), Mumbai 400 051, INDIA
T + 91 22 40700804 **F** +91 22 40700800
E info@leadstartcorp.com **W** www.leadstartcorp.com
US Office Axis Corp, 7845 E Oakbrook Circle, Madison, WI 53717, USA

All rights reserved worldwide
No part of this publication may be reproduced, stored in or introduced into a retrieval system, or transmitted, in any form, or by any means (electronic, mechanical, photocopying, recording or otherwise), without the prior permission of the Publisher. Any person who commits an unauthorised act in relation to this publication can be liable to criminal prosecution and civil claims for damages.
Disclaimer The views expressed in this book are those of the Author and do not pertain to be held by the Publisher.

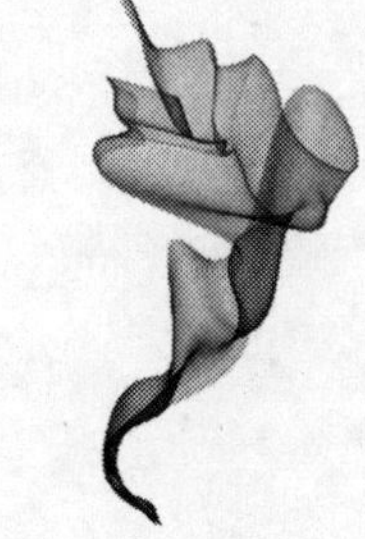

To All Spiritual Beings.

About the Author

Gian Kumar was born into a traditional Hindu family, in Burma (Myanmar). From childhood, his life held paradoxes. While he was educated at a Christian boarding school, which observed strict religious practices, these were diametrically opposed to the Hindu traditions and customs which were the norm when he went home for the holidays.

A thinker by nature, the inherent confusion and dogmas underlying religion, gradually impelled him towards spirituality. Today, he is deeply grateful for a journey filled with opportunities to learn about existential riddles such as: *Who am I? What is my purpose in Life? Is God an illusion?* Gian hopes to share his own experiential learnings with others through the medium of his books.

Gian lives with his family in New Delhi. He can be reached at: giankumar@ymail.com

---

Book I Know Thyself
Book II Think From The Heart
Love From The Mind
Book III The Ultimate Reality

Editor's Note

Repetitions, in the spiritual context, are unavoidable since the concepts are infinite while the words to describe them remain pitifully finite. In this series, the author has constantly used concepts and words such as the Absolute, Oneness, Energy, Self and so on. Besides intellectually, the author has considered the reader's need to understand and absorb the subject, step by step. Hence, the core ideas being repeated at each juncture, help the message to be distilled and internalized, instead of remaining partially understood.

It does not necessarily follow that the reader agrees with everything written. When the mind becomes impatient or restless, signalling it has understood, the reader should move on. The subjects/chapters often revolve around one word such as 'awareness' or 'oneness', which stand like the basic scale a classical *raga* is based on. Thereupon, a myriad variations and nuances are played, to attempt to convey the numerous extensions possible within the same theme.

The serious seeker of spiritualism returns by compulsion, to read again and again and hear those notes as a recurring melody, until the theme becomes clear. Like chanting a *mantra,* he then gains the proper perspective to practise what he has read.

Contents

Science defies God.
Religion isolates God.
Spiritualism sees God in all.

Preface

In today's world, it is essential to know the meaning and essence of spiritualism. When things do not work at home, with friends or at work, it is your spiritual quotient, which comes to your aid. Don't you agree that under the pretext of fulfilling desires, attachments and accumulations, we have stopped being humane? Lengthy spiritual discourses are proving to be of no use, if the essence of loving and caring for others is not inculcated.

I have often stated that most spiritual gurus, sporting different beards and special clothes are not what we need today. What we need is a simple transformation in our lives; we need to discover that subtle true self, hidden behind the constricting layers of desire, emotion and ego. We need to know, experience and realize what life and its purpose is and what that subtle sublime spirit is trying to tell us.

This book revolves around a single word: Awareness. Spiritual awareness is that level of reality, which will take you beyond the mere fact of living in the physicality of the body and mind into the realm of your consciousness. As you shift focus from the materialistic world of space-time and its measurements, as defined by science and technology, you enter a higher realm in which the focus is on experiencing and knowing your individuality. Through its thoughts, your mind can tell you all about the outer world; what is revealed, is your spirit, which enlightens you from within; making your mind aware of deeper consciousness within you, making your mind aware to be conscious by telling you, "I am, therefore I think."

Your external perception is psychophysical while your internal perception relates to empirical realization. This dimension affects you metaphysically, providing knowledge in an experiential manner, revealing that essential element called awareness or pure consciousness. Consciousness, in spiritualism, is defined as the witnessing self in purity or the ego in 'self-consciousness', forming your 'I Am'.

However, when you explore the depths of this subject, you learn that consciousness is what you really are, ultimately manifesting as 'I am That'. The focal point of this philosophy is Oneness, where God and the Devil are but separated energies in duality, stretched apart from their centre point of One, by the filters of the mind and its desires.

This book takes you to a place of higher meaning, where you find the purpose of life. It provides spiritual support to your daily interactions so that the worldly and spiritual paths unite in a wholesome manner. Your individuality dictates how you live, but here you gain knowledge on how an awareness of existential and experiential living can transform your life and lead you to fulfilment.

Based on an ancient Indian philosophy – the Science of Consciousness, this book delves into what life is all about, with respect to its relative and absolute aspects. If on one hand, we have enlightenment, then on another there is ignorance and desire; both are extremes, but play their own respective roles in our journey. Ideally, spiritual enlightenment or self-realization in pure consciousness may be the ultimate aim, but don't we all wish for a balanced, peaceful, wholesome and comfortable life?

Though this is a complex subject, I have tried to express in the best possible, what is required for us to live in a manner which is vibrant and alive, rather than indulging in the extremes of what either the materialistic world or spiritualism may demand of us. The secret to happiness lies in the degree of your spiritual awareness and personal power in handling both spiritual and material domains; how you evolve in life, your awareness and your spontaneity in the now.

Are you a blind follower of beliefs, traditions and knowledge passed down by books, teachers, parents, friends, or so-called gurus? Or, are you one of those few, who is alert, observant and aware, and analyses all things before believing what you are told, whether by a guru or any other source? These are questions you will need to ask yourself, before venturing into the field of spiritualism. Spiritualism does not require idealistic discourses or lots of learning; it only demands attention, alertness and passion in what you do and experience. Essentially, 'thinkingness' is replaced with 'knowingness'.

In the East, spiritualism is an unbroken tradition, which relies on ideas of permanence and eternity in sharp contrast to the West, dependent upon apparent impressions of body and mind, which constantly change in time and space. For this reason, spiritualism considers the existence of body and mind, to be *'Maya'* or illusory and impermanent. Life to be truly sustainable should be changeless and timeless. In our physical existence, truth and reality change with time and person concerned, making the 'truth' – deceptive, apparent, illusory and hence unreal. The word 'unreal' is not to be taken in its dictionary meaning, it has been used because of the sustainable way we think, act and look at existence in our 'me and mine' world. In our limited perceptions, we all come and go, being transitory, but never seem to realize it as we cling to emotion and illusion.

There arrives a stage in everyone's life, when you think and feel that in spite of having everything, why I am still restless and unhappy? You may have health, wealth, family and comforts; but there is something amiss. Life becomes complex, you feel that either someone is taking advantage of you or vice versa. You do not wish to give up the desire for more and more and yet you wonder, now what?

Don't you often feel disgusted or disgruntled with life, wondering what a roller coaster ride you are on? Where there is no end to yo-yoing between pleasure and pain, in the incessant desire of always wanting this or that?

Materialism, accumulations and attachments, which we all crave, make you pay, creating so many conflicts that at times you feel fed up! You pick up a book on self-development or join a spiritual or religious centre, hoping that your woes will dissipate. If you are true to yourself, you will realize however, that now, you are possibly engaged in a deeper inner conflict than ever before.

Earlier, your life was simpler than it is now, after listening to or reading all the jargon of mystical enlightenment. Because now you think you know everything, but the reverse is actually true. You love lecturing others on spirituality, but you yourself remain in the same rut of 'me, mine and myself', obsessed with ego. The reason being, you read and hear it all, but unless you practise, live, and experience to realize with that knowledge, the essence of spiritualism is not attained.

My intentions while writing and trying to express my views on the above are not to lay emphasis upon any specific Asian jargon or mystical consciousness; it is purely to benefit you and me. There may be many religious or spiritual practices in our world that serve the purpose of seeking awareness; whatever these may be, what is important is understanding, experiencing and realizing the precepts consistently. It is mainly through the study of self-realization, with gradual practice in awareness, that we can lead a more conscious life. This deeper consciousness will take us from lust to love, worry to wonder, anxiety to calmness, sadness to happiness, sorrow to joy, and from agony to celebration.

You may have to read most of what is written more than once to be able to capture the depth and intention of what I wish to express. It is also for the same reason that repetitions are necessary to drive the message home for better clarity. Decades of my life have been spent in trying to seek this reality and knowledge of truth. It is definitely not easy to absorb, unless we really want to and we should also not read such texts, if we are not serious about knowing and practising this subject.

This is the journey I wish for all of you. We are that Self, which is a part of cosmic consciousness; our bodies may disintegrate but our energy of spiritual awareness remains immortal, beyond death and destruction. This is sovereign knowledge, the secret of life, to be practised and experienced so we may rise from suffering into a life of consciousness in awareness.

In this book, there are no dictates that you need to follow, except your own; just 'be' and go with the flow in awareness. You will notice a change; an inner balance will flower and your problems will begin to dissolve naturally. Your subconscious will take over existentially, building that evolution within yourself, by yourself in living and knowing, rather than boasting of all you know. In the midst of darkness, there shall be light and in the midst of ignorance, you shall have awareness.

The lonely spirit keeps reminding you.
Life will remain lonely, sad and discontented.
Wealth and comforts,
shall keep you ignorant and incomplete.
Until you become conscious
To experience, and realize that Self.

Chapter 1
A Conscious Life
Part I

Most of us are primarily emotional. I would further add that we are slaves to our emotions and are directed by our emotional demands, as a sense of satisfaction generally comes about when our emotional desires are fulfilled. For most, there comes a stage when you start questioning your mechanical life and wonder why, in spite of having everything, you are neither contented nor fulfilled or complete within yourself. Why, do you think, is your unhappy mind constantly wandering here and there with no direction, and asking, "Now what?"

It is this emptiness, which makes you aware and then conscious of this phenomenon and you start to analyze and then embark upon a new journey to seek something apart from materialistic comforts – a life of balance, contentment, and peace. Your spiritual life commences; you begin integrating the various aspects of your life by improving your body and mind – going towards that beyond and experience what is considered to be the soul or spirit, with the objective of achieving an aware, conscious life.

Science has not yet been able to define or explain consciousness in a satisfactory manner. We all know that we experience life through the brain. Yet, for each one of us, our conscious or experiential world of thoughts and feelings differ. To each one of us, our consciousness is a separate entity; depending on our individual degree of awareness in the totality of our external and internal perceptions.

Consciousness is explained as the experience of awareness through our thoughts, perceptions, feelings, sensations, and environment. It is a mental phenomenon of insight, concentration, conviction and intention, until it becomes free to be mindful in awareness of its own individuality. Wikipedia features a quote from Stuart Sutherland's entry in the *Macmillan Dictionary of Psychology*: 'Consciousness is a fascinating but elusive phenomenon: it is impossible to specify what it is, what it does, or why it has evolved. Nothing worth reading has been written on it.'

Consciousness as a spiritual subject has been widely discussed in the Eastern world for over thousands of years. According to this philosophy, the secret of life is awareness, which is the cause of consciousness and leads to self-realization. This awareness is the all-pervasive cosmic intelligence, which is limitless, and is not bound by time or space. When this awareness merges with human matter/intelligence, it becomes the content of consciousness.

We all know that we are in a state of bliss during deep sleep, when the mind is at rest from its chattering thoughts. Is it possible to experience this bliss in our waking lives as well? We are aware of the power of our mind, which can understand and overcome our basic instincts and sensory perceptions. As you read on, you will discover that when our conscious intelligence rises above our thoughts and perceptions, we automatically elevate ourselves to a higher dimension, into the oneness of the Universe. In spiritualism, this bliss is possible upon realizing pure consciousness or total awareness, when your body and mind dissolve into the spirit as in the case of the Buddha.

Our mind is mysterious, a wonderful force, which emits our thoughts, aggressively residing and thriving in our egoistic self. Remove all thought and there will be no mind, world, perception, sensation, feeling, conscious experience or anything at all. Your world is your mind, which forms your egocentric 'I'. Your thoughts and feelings are isolated and private, forming your very own 'self-consciousness' within this intensely personal 'I'. This same mind requires awareness to perform any of its functions, as it requires the art of self-inquiry to analyze the reasons for your joy, sorrow, fear and love.

In the same manner that we learn how to specialize in various fields and excel at our professions or even keep abreast of the latest technology, it is also important to learn 'life engineering'. We are required to learn and go beyond how and what we think, to take a journey into our inner world and realize that inherent bliss and tranquillity nestled silently within. Consciousness is nothing but a series of inner experiences which your being goes through – either in ignorance or in awareness.

There are five stages in the formation of a conscious mind. It starts with the 'body consciousness' pervading each human cell. Then we have 'mind consciousness' flowing through our external sense organs, perceiving all objects from the environment. The third stage emerges from our inner perception as 'experiential-consciousness'. All this data is stored in the hard disk of our memory becoming the fourth stage, 'store-consciousness', which combines with the above three to form the 'ego' as a separate 'I'. Finally, we have the Witness Consciousness, which observes and witnesses our mind through awareness, in order for us to transcend and transform. The Witness Consciousness lies beyond the subject-object relationship and is also referred to as Pure Consciousness in Total Awareness.

We need to learn the art of disconnecting from the illusions and dualities of life that generate lust, greed, jealousy, and all sorts of negativity. We should understand the source and flow of consciousness to live in harmony with our experiences. It all depends on the seriousness of our intentions toward this subject and of course on displaying the interest and concentration required while reading the in-depth analysis provided below.

Awareness comes into play just a shade before the mind focuses its attention on any object as watcher/observer, and before any thoughts appear in the mind, activating the psychic energies of intention which help the consciousness to flow from probability to actuality. The thoughts in our mind are linked mainly to the knowledge of the past, from which we are also able to project to or construct our future. This becomes the foundation of our intellect, with which we act through memory, in the present.

As explained, our 'store consciousness' has access to our perceptual data and these perceptions are based on past experiences, which we compare and analyze through our intellect, while encountering the present. In this manner, our mind is pre-conditioned in patterns of attachment or aversion established through prior experiences. All this is merely a mental representation, an illusion, in the form of thinking or reasoning based upon self-interest and not what is real or actual. For reality to exist, it needs to be in the present moment, where your mind need not think, it just simply '*knows*'.

Thoughts originate from knowledge already gained, swinging constantly like a pendulum from the past to the future and back again, sometimes turning into emotions. Thoughts from external perceptions dilute our awareness of the present, for we mainly exist knowing about the present but not being in it, while incessantly brooding about the past or the future.

Spontaneous awareness captured by the mind in the present is what we refer to as creativity, intuition and imagination, which emerge only when we are in a 'no-mind' zone. Meaning, before our thought processes can interfere with or disturb this uncontaminated energy by thinking or analyzing it. It is derived from pure cosmic energy that merges with knowledge already gained from our sense perceptions. I would define 'creativity' as a spontaneous flash of cosmic energy, manifesting in togetherness with our mind, awakening it to a new beginning and fresh possibilities.

In spiritualism, there is no separate God; the Creator is the creation Himself. God is that Pure Consciousness or Total Awareness, the supreme energy where thoughts have no role to play; body, mind, and spirit become One. The material world claims, 'I am what I think', whereas spiritualism says, 'I am, therefore I think', which implies the spirit as you, going beyond or transcending thought.

Science cannot explain the phenomena behind consciousness. For science, facts or the object of study is the most important factor and thought tends to be viewed as a mechanical and mental process. Consciousness is abstract, it is not an object which science can cut and divide for research; it is the subject itself. It is dependent upon the level and degree of awareness manifested in an individual. Science understands consciousness as long as it is linked to our thoughts through something tangible – knowledge from the past – to make us aware of its existence.

Thoughts are the home of ego and materialism. Higher awareness in consciousness gradually enables you to ascend from your personal 'I', towards the intuitive and creative intelligence of the Absolute. You become aware of your own mind, making you conscious of your ego and its environment. This makes you realize that the luxury, power, and fame which we all crave, provides only short-term happiness, leaving behind a void that demands more and more. Those who do not inquire or probe further into life, remain caught in a vicious cycle of choices and conflicts; never knowing or understanding life and its purpose.

The role of the intellect is to have control over thought: giving it the ability to reason, control and analyze and so understand any situation objectively. Consciousness, on the other hand, is being aware to experience what is happening. In order to have consciousness, awareness has to exist – but the corollary is not necessarily true. It is awareness that gives birth to consciousness. Awareness is the sixth sense of 'knowing'. It goes beyond the five senses of perception. Awareness determines the degree of consciousness. Therefore, awareness is supreme energy, whereas consciousness is the result of the cumulative effects of experiences gained from the five senses, enlightened with awareness.

The mind needs to be aware to become conscious. Only then is an idea formed in the mind for thoughts to mull over. The mind further harnesses past awareness lodged in memory – merging with the intellect to analyse and reason. This forms the basis of your intentions to choose and indulge in any idea which your individuality or 'self-consciousness' permits.

The flow of energy emanating from this ability manifests as your intentions and the direction you choose thereon, whether it is regarding health, wealth, or the self. For example, if you are conscious of your health, your intention of improving your fitness increases. Therefore, we need to become aware of the power of consciousness. The higher this awareness, the better we get at exerting this power.

I repeat, spiritual awareness, the supreme intelligence, enters human consciousness through flashes of intuition, which forms an inner perception to ignite our minds into creative thinking by merging itself with external perception. Imagination erupts, forming an idea, ambition grows depending on the level of interest, and thoughts make their presence felt, applying knowledge already gained, along with emotions. This then triggers the intellect, the seat of reasoning and understanding, to make decisions in any situation, to be finally guided by the Witnessing Self in any particular situation. The degree of individual awareness of any situation, combined with intellect, makes it possible for consciousness to guide the above processes, completing the cycle of intention.

The above processes in our mind involve intuition, imagination, insight, conviction, concentration, emotion, induction or deduction, consciousness to infer and intention – all merging with the supreme awareness in one way or the other. This relationship of the individual 'I' with the cosmic intelligence 'I' of awareness is the reason that spiritual practices and some religions declare that God is present in all of us, stating, 'I am That'.

This awareness is in me, you and every single atom in our cosmos. The galaxy of planets, air, space, and people, all move in awareness, which is not limited by time and space. Awareness, 'I', is motionless and timeless. It is pure intelligence, present in all of us; the reason we can claim, 'I am That' – but it is independent of time and space. We are all a part of 'That' in quality, until we reach the final stage of Pure Consciousness, where body and mind dissolve in Self-realization of 'who' we really are.

When any action takes place in total awareness, it is action-less. After understanding this concept, one no longer takes credit for being the 'doer' in spite of doing. In this manner, a performer realizes that his actions are not the direct outcome of processes springing from his mind and body but from the all-pervasive awareness in the form of his Witnessing Self, as the vital substance within. Meaning, for awareness to manifest in the mind, the existence of the subject and the object are essential. This awareness is the substance, beyond and exclusive to the subject-object relationship, forming the substance of '*who*' we are.

It is almost like driving a car; you may say that you drove at one hundred miles per hour, but in reality the car was moving and your body and mind were just a part of that motion, with awareness guiding the speed at which you were going. In this way, consciousness is the source and content of the mind. It manifests in the form of body, mind, experiential, store and divine consciousness, which on realizing purity, form the Witnessing Self. It plays its role in all the dualities of life. It is awareness that keeps a check on consciousness, lifting it to the place where it can become superior and non-dual. Meaning, awareness is primary; it is the supreme achievement of the mind.

Awareness is the ultimate reality we seek. It is only through awareness that consciousness achieves its aims, becoming the source and power of the mind. Awareness is limitless energy from the universe. We may call it the divine, since both gross (matter) and subtle (mind) energy is comprised of divine consciousness as core energy. As consciousness expands through awareness, a person becomes enlightened.

Awareness is that supreme intelligence, which is omnipresent, omniscient, and omnipotent. It is present in all of us in our consciousness. 'I' as a subject, am aware of all of the objects around me, including my body and mind. Awareness is limitless, and is beyond time and space. It is absolute, because any dimension or description of time and space is only a part of this cosmos, making it relative.

This is the vision of Eastern philosophy that regardless of the limitations of your body and mind, consciousness, awareness or divinity can manifest itself by merging itself with your mind and body. Hence, you are a part of that divine consciousness. '*Tat tvam asi*' means 'I am That'' or 'That Thou Art', signifying that you are one with God yourself; one needs self-realization to become aware, experience and realize enlightenment.

Awareness can be acquired in several ways – one may achieve it through knowledge, experience, or intuition. However, in this context, awareness is mainly related to self-realization or an inner transformation. It maps the journey, which starts with discovering that we are limited in our mental capacity and trapped in ignorance. The ignorance of our own selves believing that we are the doers makes us live in the illusion of dualities and dichotomies, suffering from fear, sorrow, and contempt. We ordinarily remain detached from a universal awareness of oneness and live in a world of our own: me, mine, and myself. Even God has been invented by our limited minds for our own convenience. Reaching for awareness relates to the supreme knowledge that you as object; body and mind and God as the subject, both having absolute energy as the constituent, are the same, and you should become aware and live within the collective consciousness of this Oneness to be in bliss.

Scientists are of the view that our universe or cosmos is made of matter/energy, which implies the mind emerges out of gross physical matter, and consciousness is a by-product of the electrochemical functions of the mind. For scientists, consciousness is a neural activity but they have not been able to explain how even a simple experience is born.

Spiritualism postulates that this all-prevalent cosmic energy manifests in the mind as awareness, to make the mind aware, in order to generate consciousness for the body to experience and realize. As the consciousness of this awareness increases, the divinity within us rises. This transcendence ultimately enables us to go beyond the realm of our external thoughts into a thoughtless zone, in complete awareness of the divine, which is referred to as Total Awareness.

This means we are, in fact, a small part of the cosmic divine intelligence or awareness, undergoing a physical human experience, comprised of an eternal mixture of absolute energy in the form of matter. Endowed with human form, we are made of body and mind, seen and felt by the perception of our senses, and prone to changes; but the overall energy remains constant in its continuity. In this way, the Universe constantly evolves in its eternal free-flowing energy, in a cycle of birth and death, from an embryo in the foetus to its disintegration, dissolving back to where it came from, taking different shapes and forms, like plants, animals or humans.

Therefore, it is awareness that reveals your presence when it merges with mental energy, forming the content of consciousness, energizing the force of life. We should keep in mind what science tells us – everything in this universe — solid, fluid or gas — is all encompassed in an enormous unified field of energy in continuum. It may change its form, but remains constant overall. Our five senses perceive a human to be a part of this absolute energy, in the guise of what is referred by us as the 'Universe', which is limited in time and space, and designed to objectify this as physical reality. Accordingly, 'I' as an individual is just a perception of our limited mind restricted to the frequencies and vibrations of our energy system.

Man is a burden on his consciousness.
With conditions, concepts and choices.
He forgets the real Self in favour of his false self.

Part II

The mind, using its three-dimensional perceptions, creates a world of its own; sub-atomically it consists (according to the theory of quantum energy) of electrons, protons, and neutrons. Einstein suggested that we are all essentially one; matter and energy are interchangeable. Therefore, even scientifically, all creatures and objects may seem disconnected from one another perceptually, but in reality, we are all part of one continuous flow of energy. The area which science is unaware of is what we know as the language of experience and consciousness

– the domain of the spirit where mysticism reigns. The universe talks to us in one language, it prepares one to realize and recognize awareness in all of its manifestations in nature. Our thinking, which is driven by self-interest, dilutes this awareness, so much so that we have nearly destroyed our environment.

If we pay attention, we will notice that our thoughts not only affect us but also everyone around and beyond. As long as we remain isolated in our own conceptual thoughts, we stagnate in individual consciousness and suffer. However, when we tune in positively with society as a whole, we take part in collective consciousness and thrive with peace. As individuals, we have a tendency to cut, divide and analyze, seeking gain only for ourselves, destroying the true essence of nature. However, when we function in unison, as a part of this one existence, we simply flow with life.

We may think that we are free but our individuality or uniqueness is minimal when compared to the effect of generations of conditioning from family, society, community and those who rule us. In fact our subconscious, the storehouse of our memory or consciousness, functions in conditioned reflex action mode, many a times involuntarily, without the permission of the mind. Once you have learned how to drive, swim or walk, you do not require the active participation of the mind to undertake these tasks.

Our consciousness is also deeply interconnected with the collective consciousness. Our likes and dislikes are dependent on the way others see things. When many, collectively say a thing is beautiful or fashionable, we generally accept this as being true, signifying that our consciousness is a part of the same whole. Therefore, we can rely only on our own awareness and the Witnessing Self as the Pure Consciousness, when it witnesses through observation to inform us otherwise, when we discriminate and choose. This is what transforms and upgrades the mind, in forming our individuality.

If breath is what brings life into the body, it is awareness which ignites the mind to become conscious of how to think, act, experience and realize. Raw energy, after manifesting in the mind, becomes aware and is utilized differently by each of us, depending on the level of awareness achieved and the degree of collective consciousness that prevails. Collective consciousness should not be underestimated. To give an example of this unified field and its power, think of the force of energy of a football match. You find thousands of people collectively cheering for their team in continuity. Similarly, on the other end, a frenzy can be seen during rioting, when people collectively lose their mental control.

Life is not a goal; it is a journey to be lived with purpose. The purpose is to live in joy with awareness, and to do so collectively. Goals are for individuals, who compete to achieve results to prove they are smarter than others. This may be necessary when one is young but with maturity and age, one should transform and gain a higher awareness of our consciousness. The essence of life is full of the collective aggregation of this supreme energy called love.

We all know and realize that life is not easy or transparent. All of us want success and wealth. We may not accept it, but as we climb the ladder of life we become so much like animals, snatching and looting as much as we can, but always in denial of doing so. We become enmeshed in the paradigm of the law of the jungle – 'survival of the fittest'. Think about it, is this how and what life should be? Is this the complete story or do we need to learn more and go beyond our normal mechanical, materialistic life and taste the real happiness of peace and contentment?

A seeker of awareness realizes the ignorance behind the continual desire of wanting more and more and wishes to liberate himself from a prison of his own making. When conscious intelligence develops, he tries to become aware and integrates his consciousness by bringing together his body, mind and spirit with supreme awareness of what is around and inside. He welcomes a life of detachment from worldly desires, entering a journey of freedom and contentment, free of contempt, jealousy, and hatred. This is living a conscious life.

Yoga and meditation are techniques one can practice to reach this divine consciousness. Yoga should never be taken as merely physical exercise or breath control; these are simply one part of yoga. At the deeper level, yoga means union or fusion, the union of the self with divine or cosmic power. Mind-body-soul merge, taking you beyond mere existence in body and mind to unite you with Absolute Reality. This has been exemplified in various yoga combinations of *Jnana* yoga (knowledge), *Karma* yoga (selfless action), *Dhyan* yoga (meditation), and *Bhakti* yoga (devotion), all leading to what is called *Anand* yoga (bliss).

Such a journey finally leads to experiencing and realizing God as '*Sat-chit-anand*': '*sat*' means to be in existence, '*chit*' to be in pure consciousness, and '*anand*' to be in bliss. Meditation too leads us toward divine consciousness, away from our individual thoughts, as explained in detail later.

Of all the types of yoga, it is said that *Kundalini* yoga is the highest form. It encompasses physical, mental, and spiritual discipline for developing strength, awareness, character, and consciousness. It is called the yoga of awareness. It is an advanced form of yoga and meditation. Its purpose is to cultivate the creative spiritual potential for attaining self-realization to ultimately merge into God-consciousness.

Absolute Reality is eternal and unchangeable, having no distortion. It exists beyond time, space, and individuality, with full awareness of cosmic energy and intelligence. In fact, reality normally exists at three levels: absolute, empirical and illusory. The reality of non-duality is infinite and of non-dual consciousness of being, referred to as 'I am' or the Absolute. It is extremely rare to realize such reality in consciousness and is not meant for the average person.

Empirical reality is that which is experiential, the phase in which we normally exist; it appears real at certain times and vice-versa, changing its appearance (God-Devil, Good-Bad, Happiness-Sorrow, etc.) and being constrained by time and space. For instance, for truth to exist, lies have to be a part of our relative life. Finally, there is illusory reality – those things, which have no existence apart from hallucinations or acts of erroneous imagination.

A higher state of consciousness arises through the intensity of our awareness. If this is positive, then the world around us falls into patterns of serenity, calmness, and harmony. The space between and around our thoughts is what brings everything to oneness. We can experience this heightened state of awareness, if we wish to, for short periods of time through Transcendental Meditation.

However, there were sages in India who practised this at the highest level of intensity, to reach a state called '*Samadhi*'. This means that for a specified period of time, they gave up all human consciousness, where time and space were of no consideration to them. They were not attached to any phenomenon of the mind and body and were able to reach a state of complete fullness and perfection, dissolving in spiritual radiance with the oneness of the Universe, in divine sleep.

Unfortunately, we remain largely unaware of the power of consciousness. This is why we are not aware of 'who' we really are and of the potential power that lies within us. If we make use of even a fraction of this power, we will be able to experience the wonders of existence, without having to resort to illusions like anger, hatred, jealousy, lust, etc. This will teach us how to live collectively in synchronicity, wherein we will discover that things happen automatically in response to our inner peace and balance. The secret of personal power is awareness of that power; only then can you manifest this power. In this manner, a conscious life brings together our body, mind, and spirit; experientially, to be present in the presence of each and every moment, living with awareness of what is inside and around us.

In history, we have the outstanding case of Dr. Viktor Frankl, the famous Austrian psychiatrist and his experiences in a concentration camp during the Second World War. His awareness of the power to choose, feel, and decide could not be altered by his Nazi captors, in spite of all the humiliation and torture to which he was subjected. He was aware enough to decide, within himself, how all of this was going to affect him. He realized that his freedom of choice to bear all the pain and suffering was far greater than the freedom of those soldiers who were inflicting such pain. He said, "Between stimulus and response there is a space. In that space is our power to choose our response. In that response lie our growth and our freedom."

Our life is based on desires, choices, ambition and wants, which never end. This is how we struggle throughout our life, accumulating and merely following cause and effect in result orientation. From one idea, thought and desire to another, life goes on. Accumulations and attachments continue and the struggle leads to success and failure. We get judged by the outside world by what we have and not by who we are.

What we need is to find the truth behind the constant desire and ambition to 'become' something. We need awareness because without awareness, mere mechanical accumulations lead to the decay of the mind, reducing happiness and creating emptiness within. Do not discard choice or want, but become aware enough of yourself not to be blindly driven towards anything. This will take you toward a path of self-fulfilment where there is less struggle and conflict.

In relation to the above, operate the laws of 'Karma', influenced by thought, speech and action. When we function through 'mind consciousness', karmas are linked to the concept of cause and effect. If related to destiny, our karmas in collective or associative consciousness succumb and become victim to our circumstances. In mindfulness, living from one moment to the next, in observance and awareness, destiny does not have a role to play. The perceiver and the perceived become one. The subject and the object exist in unison with the substance: awareness. Reality emerges existentially in the presence of the now, when you do not need to perceive, think, reason or infer; you simply know – that is how we refer to truth and reality.

Most of us respond to experiences in life without enough awareness and by forgetting this radiance. Further, this reactive tendency weakens us, as it is said, 'no one can hurt you without your consent'. You are what you are because of the choices that you made. If the choices have been reactive, you will be prone to conditioned responses, to a life steeped in dualities, with choices leading to conflicts in the mind that evoke feelings of anger, fear, or jealousy. You will blame others for your doings, and all this will finally result in regret, repentance and resentment.

However, if your choices have been proactive, your intellect will be guided by awareness, responding to various stimuli creatively. You will be in a position to act not only in a way which benefits you but is in accordance with the actuality of that situation, in the presence of the now. This will make you alert and observant (minus thoughts) of your speech and actions – the what, where and when – in that divine manner – of what is expected of us.

When we absorb this understanding and knowledge of the power of awareness, we will bring about a transformation in our lives. Our purpose in life will change from the dualities of choices and conflicts to that of an auto-flow of awareness. In any situation you will pause, take a deep breath and be calm; you will not always wish to 'win the argument' or fight to prove that your opinion was correct or get pleasure from hurting a person who has harmed you. You will want to bring about a favourable outcome for any issue. You will want to be fair to all, exist in collective harmony, and have better relationships. Awareness will simply make you conscious of why you say 'yes' or 'no' – so simple, yet so important.

When you are in the presence of the moment,
the essence of thought loses its significance.

Chapter 2
What is Meditation?
Part I

The spiritual journey of any seeker can only begin after he is able to comprehend the knowledge of the inner Witnessing Self in knowing the reality of 'Who am I'. He would be able to understand the possibility of going beyond his physical self into another dimension. This is where meditation emerges; to act as a counterpoint to your thoughts, which drive you into materialism. Meditation can calm, relax and soothe your mind to help you enter a different dimension.

Meditation is a state of discipline, in which you detach your mind to reach a stage where you are observing in alertness with all awareness but without thinking or needing to think. When the consciousness in a man detaches itself from the objects, which the mind perceives, it is referred to as a state of 'thoughtless awareness'.

In the West, meditation is practiced as a concentrated effort to suppress the mind into inactivity. The intention being to calm, relax and heal the body and mind. In the East, meditation was introduced thousands of years ago to dissolve the mind into a higher state of observance or watchfulness to be more in the knowing state rather than the thinking state, in order to enact any activity effortlessly in awareness.

You will notice that many a times such a state arises in us when say, we are watching an action-packed game. The whole body responds spontaneously in awareness to what is happening, but without giving the mind any time to think. This produces results, which are far more intense, transforming your capability and individuality in the spontaneity of the now.

There are three basic aspects to meditation. The first is spiritual revival for any person to connect to the infinite, the eternal spirit of oneness or the real Self. The second is to submerge the mind in deep concentration through chanting, mantras and various breathing techniques for a defined reason. The third is living in meditation with mindfulness in thoughtless awareness, with full acceptance to transform oneself.

Meditation was introduced in those ancient days to discipline the mind. This was done by closing the eyes in order to turn the mind inwards. To attain intuitive knowledge of the Self one had to plunge inwards and restrict words and thoughts and inputs from the sensory organs. For this purpose, one had to sit quietly, close the eyes and meditate upon the syllable '*Om*': the all-pervading divine energy representing the united aspects of the creator, preserver and the liberator in a vibratory mantra.

While meditating on the Self, the meditator meditating through the mind on meditation becomes one and the same because he is nothing but a part of that subject, separated and differentiated only by thoughts and words. This process starts with '*Dhyana*', meaning concentration and ends in *Samadhi* — the highest stage possible in meditation, in which a person experiences oneness with the Universe. When the experience (subject), experiencing the experienced (object) becomes one, the experiencing (mind) disappears.

Meditation as a way of living in mindfulness (living in heightened awareness from one moment to the next) was also introduced during those days, in the form of various methods of attaining awareness by silencing the mind in observation, alertness and acceptance of all that exists. These are centring techniques to gather the separated energies of duality back into oneness.

These methods are meant to take you beyond the limitations of the mind, which normally function in dichotomies through abstract thinking. Meditation, whatever the purpose, leads to the same destination: to be conscious, to live in the now and search for the absolute truth, away from our perceptual thoughts.

Meditation was first discovered in India. We know this through ancient scriptures with the documented history of many thousands of years; much before any religion came into existence, under the doctrine of *'Vigyan Bhairav Tantra'* where 112 meditative techniques were provided covering every aspect of meditation. These involved practices in breathing, chanting mantras, visualization, contemplation, concentration, mindfulness and many others. No study or research upon meditation is complete, unless one goes through these, well explained, all-inclusive meditative techniques.

No guru can cultivate, enliven or enlighten the meditation process or awareness within you. It should be a living awareness and not an imposed one. However, in some cases, you may induce or bring about abrupt changes in your mind and body through Transcendental Meditation or a few other meditation techniques; the information pertaining to which is available in abundance today. These techniques have been devised to suit various gurus' own branding and institutions, promising you the stars and the moon. The results that you realize in such cases are but temporary.

You soon revert to your own reactive physical self, drowning in the same chaos of the mind.

Such techniques should be considered as therapy for mental relaxation only, providing short-term benefits, rather than befitting the purpose for which meditation was conceived. However, they do have certain health benefits, from cardiovascular to the extra release of the telomerase enzyme, which increases the life expectancy of telomeres, which play an important role in cell division and longevity.

What we really need is meditation in utter spiritual awareness within the presence of the now; spontaneously. Not by sitting in a corner, suppressing our thoughts, trying to control our mind for a short time. Consciousness here plays an important role, for in order to exist, each of us has to be aware of both the outer and inner worlds. Consciousness, when exposed to the material world loses its purity, plunging into the dualities of existence rather than staying nearer its origin – awareness.

Consciousness is all-important as it is the perceiver for the sense organs, experiencer for the mind and thinker for the intellect. In order to perform all these functions, consciousness needs to be aware to become conscious — the reason for energy to manifest into awareness. It is only in purity that they meet in parity, a state considered to be the fifth dimension. One proceeds from the third to the fourth and then to the fifth dimension, reviving one's consciousness, in order to reach the stage of purity or absolute non-dual awareness.

Spiritual awareness can be attained through discipline of the mind, which is maintained when the mind rises above its incessant chattering in dualities, and its craving for desires and attachments. For this, meditation alone is the answer. Meditation is a process — one practices inner discipline to focus on one single subject or object in exclusion, stemming all other flow of thoughts. One can easily summarize that meditation is awareness and vice versa.

To develop awareness, we start with our mind being alert and observant. It is important not to ponder upon the past and future, but observe the present.

It essentially starts with watchfulness; not to react from impressions embedded in memory but to observe in awareness with alertness and accept the present situation in its totality.

In order to start a life of living with awareness in the now, we need to meditate. We need to become proactive rather than being reactive. The aim is not to impose meditation upon ourselves, but to live naturally from one moment to the next meditatively. Watching, looking at and observing the present moment in alertness, in order to accept both dualities with grace. Outgrow what you don't approve of and transform into something fresh, spontaneously. This way of living in meditation is nothing but being in the presence of the now in awareness.

The reason we should meditate is not just to go inwards or still the mind. The mind can never be silent for too long; thoughts are an automatic consequence of any interest shown by the mind, activating its memory bank to analyze, discern, and choose. As long as any interest or desire is present, the mind remains active.

The intention of meditation is to detach from this interest and observe neutrally. Then there will be fewer thoughts in emotions to disturb the body. One should note and remember that even if the mind or thoughts are merely quiet, karmic performance continues with less obstruction and 'thinkingness' becomes replaced with 'knowingness' through sheer observation.

We need to meditate to change and transform our attitudes towards life effortlessly, with awareness. We have so much knowledge and belief in the high ideals of sacredness and righteousness, through the thoughts and words that spring from the mind, but our way of living reflects just the opposite. Mediation in awareness is that discipline, in which belief and action become one. There is a distinct realization to change, outgrow and transform in awareness, by not approving involuntarily any wrongdoing in our actions. Otherwise, we continue to feel, think and only brood when we have done something wrong and in many cases repeat the mistake in ignorance.

If we are to reach the real Self, thoughts on intuition in awareness are required to take over the thoughts of perception, so all the three: body, mind and soul function as one. Such meditative methods can only be followed while remaining in a state of mindfulness: by living in full awareness from one moment to the next. The aim is to be close to the presence of our being in the now, rather than allowing the perceptive mind to brood about the past and the future.

Tantra means methods of living in meditation, through observation, acceptance and awareness. It is to flow with life, to accept and relate to our creativity and intuition in effortless awareness, from where imagination emerges. Acceptance implies total acceptance — the realization that God and the Devil, truth and untruth are one and not two. To become aware in grace and outgrow what you do not approve of without thinking, without the mind playing a major role.

Therefore, unlike yoga where effort is required, *tantra* meditation is living in awareness and accepting any situation to accomplish a spiritual goal, connecting to your core, and expanding your consciousness towards oneness, effortlessly. *Tantra* demands awareness, meditation and acceptance, in the presence of the now. The primary direction of *tantra* is – do not classify anything as right or wrong, accept all in awareness; adjust to the now and live in the moment to express yourself in mindfulness.

The only difference between yoga and *tantra* is that in yoga you need to make an effort to achieve your desired result. In *tantra,* the results are achieved seamlessly in awareness, with you outgrowing naturally those factors, which you do not approve of without making any effort. For example, if you need to stop smoking, do not criticize or negate the habit. Accept that you smoke, and be aware every time you do so. In this repeated and regular watchfulness, an inner awakening – through your past awareness of knowledge – will blossom in your consciousness. You will effortlessly outgrow the habit and chances are high that you will eventually stop it as well.

The process of centring in meditative techniques, where both extremes of duality are brought closer toward their oneness, is explained in detail in my third book on existential or experiential realization titled, *The Ultimate Reality*. The reason for these meditative techniques is that energy or spirit is all that exists and cannot remain in separation into dualities for long.

This absolute energy achieves equilibrium only in one entity and not when they are divided as two. In dual living the mind is separated into opposites or extremes to discriminate and choose on the basis of self-interest. These dualities are to be respectfully brought back to their centre in self-awareness. Otherwise, the mind and its perceptive thoughts will exist only in dualities, creating conflicts, despair, anxiety and suffering.

Timelessness is the no-mind zone.
The fountain of creativity, truth, love, reality and awareness is the source of meditation.

Part II

Meditation is 'sadhana' (a practice to accomplish a goal in spirituality), which can take you towards a state of peace and tranquillity. Meditation is for everybody, irrespective of whether you believe in God, the soul, etc. or not. To meditate is to go inwards, it merely needs that quietening of your chattering thoughts for you to experience and realize who you are. In meditation there is no need for words, language, logic or reason. You need be just as you are. Simply practice acceptance – watching, looking and observing in alertness, but minus your thoughts.

Meditation is most useful to remind you of 'who you are'. Most of our mental problems originate from being confused about our real identity. Once you realize: 'I am That', awareness floods in, which is in continuity with the concept of all as one. Until we reach that final stage of reviving that completeness, our 'self-consciousness' remains separate in a state of ego-consciousness. We remain stagnant, with a shallow outward identity, sustained only by self-interest and ego, with an external name, a physical body and a mechanical mind tied to religion and social bonds.

The meaning of life lies in going beyond such limitations. Be aware, realize, and flow in continuous ecstasy of your higher consciousness. Every man/woman lives for the future and that is why he/she does not know the meaning of life. They may think they live, but they only pretend to; for their hopes and desires never end, for desires do not reside in the now. The meaning of desire always relates to wanting something in the future.

Both Vedanta and *Tantra* stress upon a twofold life. In its four requisites for life, the former stresses on achieving prosperity in wealth through righteousness, and to fulfil desires in order to eventually understand and follow the path of liberation. If there were no material world, the need for a spiritual life would not arise. Therefore it is through our worldly life that we need to arise into the sphere of spiritual perfection. Similarly, *Tantra* signifies spiritual or meditative awareness to accept and enjoy life in all its aspects — materialistic and spiritual, but in oneness. You need to understand life in its totality and not just in discreet parts. You need to enjoy everything that you do, whether you are eating or making love. You need to minimize diverse thoughts and maximize awareness of your presence, in what you are doing.

Life is lived most fully in spiritual awareness and unconditional love to retain the spirit of totality and oneness. Therefore, living is meant to be lived in the now, because it is all that exists; one moment to the next. Live in mindfulness, be observant, alert and aware but in acceptance of the totality of any situation. This sort of living is called meditation.

Meditation is to realize the now, as it is and not be entwined in thoughts of the future or the past, the way the mind wishes to be. Meditation is a living process of action in alertness and watchfulness – witnessing and realizing, merging the past, present and future in one experiential and existential continuum.

There are various shortcuts prescribed for meditation, the most popular one is Transcendental Meditation (TM). It is a palliative like aspirin, giving you temporary relief but not a cure. It is very popular, because it is brief, relaxing, and convenient. It also inflates your ego by making you feel and say, "I am a meditator". Its primary appeal seems to be to the ego.

TM makes you feel that you have achieved something. You need to make an effort in order to relax. True mediation is just the opposite, as it requires you to simply watch, look and observe in alertness to become aware, effortlessly; to witness, as your consciousness does, whether you are still or in motion. You watch yourself and your environment, being focused, without thinking and judging, but in the presence of the now.

In a meditative state you will automatically outgrow what you do not approve of. Your efforts in observing more and thinking less and becoming aware will transform into something fresh, new and creative. The mind, which draws data from the past, has no capacity for grasping the truth as truth can only be experienced and realized in the now. It has no means of creative output, for that requires not past knowledge but fresh, spontaneous intelligence of the now. The thoughts in the mind are only a repetition of old data fed into it.

It is spiritual awareness, which brings forth something new, spontaneously, in the form of creativity, intuition and imagination. The same awareness gets converted into thoughts and merges with intellect and reason, from which logic arises. Meditation is a state of being without thought. It is a way of spiritual living, which gives rise to intuition, making you alive, sensitive and non-judgmental. Meditation, because of its various benefits, has been linked to religion. In reality, it is pure and simple awareness of the mind.

Thoughts, because they relate only to the past or the future are mechanical and repetitive. When the mind is silent or asleep, the vibrations in the mind operate at lower frequencies or wavelengths. In meditation, even though we are awake, as the mind becomes stiller, it enables the humming of thoughts to settle at a lower frequency. This level is referred to as the mind being in theta level where brainwaves range in a calming zone from 4–8 Hz.

In this state, the mind is said to be in a deeper state of awareness with better intuitive and imaginative powers. Since meditation has many mental and health benefits, it has been widely researched by science and now many new techniques have been introduced from all over the world. However, *'Vigyan Bhairav Tantra'* the most ancient text is still a valuable document. 112 meditation techniques are provided in it, meant to address every aspect of silencing the mind and centring the self, back into the One. It provides specific methods suitable to any practitioner of any age.

Meditation, like happiness, is a state of being. You need to create that state naturally. Spiritual awareness is a flow of energy, which cannot be forced. It has to flow from your natural self and transform your consciousness to reach a higher level. *Tantra* is a method to practice with awareness, so that achieving higher states of being becomes effortless.

Meditation suits the person who is settled in his mind. Who is comfortable with his surroundings, like a free bird in the sky and not in a cage? Not like the padres, monks and pundits dressed up in their uniforms in religious places. These acolytes have suppressed all their wants and desires: of money, sex and materialism. Controlling or renouncing materialistic desires is surely suppression by the mind, though that desire is bound to remain and throb deep within.

Living with awareness in the world of materialism is far more required and more practical now than it might have been thousands of years before. Similarly, when we have spiritual awareness, sex loses its physical lust; it inhabits the state of sacredness of becoming One.

The aim of meditation is honing one's awareness for joy, not the suppression of the mind. Use your mind, never negate it. It is the most powerful computer you can imagine. Use it like a machine, as a slave but never be used by it. Do not let it become your master. Use the mind, meaning perceptual thoughts, only for the materialistic world, to attain wealth and comforts but forget about it when you are alone – be in a no-mind zone.

Your mind should be at rest and awareness watching in alertness, doing its job with joy rather than in desire. This is why holidays are so joyful and invigorating, because your mind functions in a meditative wavelength, in lower vibrations and frequencies. The anxious mind has been put to rest, and that is what meditation is all about. Every day should be a holiday.

In the gap between the experiencer and the experienced, there is a space, where the process of experiencing through the mind takes place. This space is reserved for the mind to act; it is for you to fill this space, either in reactive mode to a stimulus through your thoughts or in proactive mode through meditation in awareness.

The moment you become aware of your mind, you change; you become the witness and not the thought. So you can either choose to be the witness in awareness, or the mind constantly in thoughts of desire and want. The role of experiencing by the experiencer is most crucial. It cannot be done just by practicing TM. I repeat, it is either your real self, the aware witness, or your false self, the ego, which represents your personality.

You will realize the difference when meditation is a part of your life. Your mind is to be exercised in the now, because awareness occurs only in the presence of the now. It needs to be practised from moment to moment. TM is only a flavour or taste of what mediation actually is. Meditation is the flow of awareness in the fourth dimension – the sixth sense – and the key to life. With *Sadhana* or spiritual meditation, this key opens the door to the real you.

Take the case of two strangers meeting one another. The first smiles and the other returns the smile with courtesy, seeing a calm, serene and simple man. The first man then introduces himself, revealing his name and from that identity, the other person gets an idea about his religion and nationality. The first then gives his credentials revealing his position in society. There is an immediate mental analysis and psychic waves are disturbed, the mind comes into beta or hyperactive level. The mind decides whether the smile should be retained or brushed off. This is the crucial difference between meditation and perceptive thoughts of the mind. Meditation is nothing but knowing you, without reference to the perceptual mind. In the meditative state one does not analyze in self-interest but accepts in awareness.

Life has to be taken as a game, it is an interesting cosmic joke, whether one likes it or not, and whether spiritual gurus agree or not. They should understand that dissolving our body, mind and intellect to merge with the soul in self-realization or total awareness is not what we wish for in our mortal existence. Probably, only one in a billion human beings realizes enlightenment like Buddha or Jesus and that too after hundreds or thousands of years. What we need in our daily lives is that inner balance where there is inspiration, intuition, integrity and intention in spiritual awareness. What we should seek more than anything else, is to realize fulfilment in life in a wholesome manner where there is a balance achieved between material and spiritual existence.

Meditation is supposed to fill that gap to reveal the fourth dimension. The presence of the now tells us, don't think, be still, observe and relax. There is no reason for you to be anxious, or torn between right or wrong, this and that or mine and yours. Just be aware, indulge and enjoy. Enjoyment should be your purpose; enjoyment should be your meditation. Whatever you do, enjoy doing it not mechanically but meditatively, whether it is music, dance, sex or prayer. This way, creativity will follow and your imagination will surpass your thoughts and take you forward in leaps and bounds.

Life is linear existence. On one end you have a mind with never-ending desires acting in its self-interest and on the other is pure consciousness. Awareness lies in the centre, as a pivot to balance the two. Your intention, through consciousness decides which side to tilt towards, either in separation through relativity or to bring the two dualities closer towards their centre of oneness in awareness. Only by witnessing do you realize what a roller-coaster ride in pleasure and pain the mind takes you on.

In the centre is that point where both these energies meet. The energy has been separated into dualities or dichotomies. In order for the mind to exist, everything needs to be related to its opposite. It is the job of awareness to make you consciously bring them back to their meeting point, which is what fulfilment, totality and completeness is all about.

The purpose of life is to listen, not to one extreme of any duality, but to both, because in fact both are one and not two, they have only been separated by the mind. They may move in separate directions, they may not have similarities but they are like two arms or legs of the same body. You need both for proper living. If you tilt towards one, say only towards materialism, you are bound to suffer. Tilting too much towards the other side is also an obsession. Once you understand that left cannot exist without right, your perception changes. In reality there is no separation. It is all One.

The way you see monks trying to control their minds by chanting, shaving their heads, wearing saffron clothes – they seem to be fooling themselves. Let them loose in a mall, discotheque or a public place and notice the glee and awe evident in them. Life is not meant to be lived by renouncing, suppressing and controlling. Centring these two separated energies, caused due to duality, back into oneness, in acceptance of both, increases the energy levels within us. We are to respect both, treating spiritual awareness as the inner God and our attachments in desire as the Devil.

We need balance to evolve in that presence, where on one hand we have health, wealth and comforts and on the other humility, compassion and selflessness. We need to relate to both dimensions in balance. We need to be alive, love and forgive others and our self. This inner and outer balance is the purpose of life that I wish for all of you. Be alert, accept both yourself and the given situation; your energy will centralize and there will be less conflict. Do not negate anything as that is a waste of energy.

Spiritualism says one needs to be desire-less. *Tantra* says do not negate desire; accept and indulge, but with full awareness. 'Desirelessness' would be an act of control or renouncement, leading to suppression. Acceptance in full consciousness will make you outgrow that which is not appropriate for you. As long as thoughts exist, there will be desires, ego and attachments, for that is how the mind is designed; suppression is not the answer, spiritual awareness or meditation is the key.

Remember on one side, if you wish for desire then on another, there should be dispassion. In *tantra* there is total acceptance. It is actually your objective mind, which divides the total energy into two, good and bad, but it is your subjective consciousness, which ultimately decides what to accept and indulge in. In awareness, everything just happens, you do not surrender, sheer acceptance takes place.

Meditation is not a process of reducing mind activity. It is efficacious to transform your thoughts of separation into thoughts of acceptance in awareness. The difference between yoga and meditation is that in yoga you need to make an effort with discipline and an effort to experience and realize something that you want. Meditation is just the opposite. In meditation, you need to be awake but in a no-mind state, observing with alertness, and being aware of what you are watching.

Transcendental Meditation requires effort, it becomes something of a yogic exercise to sleep and relax, separating or focusing, repeating a word to distract the mind. This repeating or focusing, makes you drowsy, reduces your brain waves to come down from beta to the theta levels. This is not real or spiritual mediation, it is a psychic application or an effort to reduce the vibrations and frequencies of your brain waves.

Mediation is *tantra*, a technique to quieten the mind, not by making it drowsy but by making it aware and reducing thoughts to reach total acceptance. This way there is less conflict when positives and negatives are brought closer towards their centre. It is a centring technique. This is the difference between relaxation and meditation. Relaxation tends to make your mind drowsy. Meditation is the science of consciousness to take you beyond thoughts into awareness. TM takes you into a state of dreaming, whereas spiritual meditation takes you towards reality. However, both reduce brain waves because the frequencies decrease, one by resting and the other by increased awareness.

The first few techniques in '*Vigyan Bhairav Tantra*' are about how to become aware through breathing. It is done in watching your inhalation and exhalation. After Lord Shiva, who introduced meditation, we had the Buddha, thousands of years later. He was one of the first few to have mastered these techniques of meditation to be conferred the title of 'the awakened one'. Later, various other meditative techniques and exercises were introduced in China, Japan and Korea.

Meditation makes you observe reality as it is. It brings you out of the state of dreaming. Throughout our lives, we live within the illusions wrought by our sensory organs, dreaming of and desiring a world, which eludes us by constantly changing into this or that. We require awareness to understand this ignorance of our false self and awaken to the reality of truth, love and the presence of our being.

The reality of your dreams is your existence in body and mind. The reality of your awakening is that presence in awareness, where you come to realize who and what you are and practice total acceptance accordingly.

Religion says that God as the Creator is a separate entity and that you will either go to heaven or hell as per your deeds in life. The second school of Hindu thought, the oldest philosophy or religion known to man, claims that the Creator is none other than the Creation. Heaven and hell are experienced by our deeds in this very life. We transgress or transmigrate, from one existence into another, until we realize pure consciousness in total awareness. It is entirely up to you and your awareness, consciousness and intellect, what you may wish to believe or follow.

God cannot be comprehended, by the eyes, words, rituals or by temples, churches or mosques. The one God may only be realized through consciousness, awareness and oneness.

Chapter 3
Mind of God

This title may seem absurd and the subject elaborated upon may challenge our conditioning, our pre-determined beliefs or traditional faith. It goes to a space science and religion have not been able to touch upon – the basic question of how to free our minds from the incessant chatter of our thoughts, which lead to anxiety, fear, contempt and sadness. Detailed within this chapter is an antidote to our entire set of negative habits, from lust to greed; something beyond, yet so simple, which God within wishes to share, trying to tell us – my mind is your mind.

The only condition is to free yourself of the thousands of years of propaganda of cult, creed and culture or of multimillion-dollar religious or spiritual organizations, where you remain weak, locked in the cages of religious beliefs – Hindu, Christian or Moslem. Consider how you can get out of this bondage, liberate yourself and become mentally strong and be able to share, moment by moment, something beyond physical thought, language and the mind, transcending the ordinary to reach fresh intelligence-energy. I am sure you will realize this can help solve one of the biggest problems of humankind – of how to use your mind, instead of being used by it.

Day-to-day choices, decisions, comparisons, conflicts, reacting to this or that, mainly result in you condemning others. Instead of that, become choice-less, where you are neither for something nor against it. You accept every situation with grace, in the sheer awakening of your awareness in the presence of the now. Materialism and spiritualism meet at this crossroads, where decisions are taken through consciousness.

This whole chapter is based on what I have learned

and gathered from ancient Indian philosophy about life and its existence. According to these teachings, whatever you perceive through your sensory organs is apparent and illusory, meaning – they seem real but are not real, being short-lived impressions of your mind, which keep changing.

These external perceptions are dependent on dualities, dichotomies or are relative to one another, providing cycles of pleasure and pain, love and hatred, happiness and sadness and so on. You may objectively see, feel and taste reality, but only for a short while. Nothing is permanent; the real can change into the unreal, depending on the perceptual mind. It is only when you transcend thoughts, sensory perceptions and emotions, that you become alive to the realities of life.

Reality, like the sky and ocean, is subjective. It has no beginning or end, being neither divisible nor dependent on our perceptions. Our sensory organs can perceive reality only as an object or as a part of a subject. It is our mind, which is divided into three parts: the first is the sense of sensory perception; in the second we have the supra-sensory perceptions of our experiences forming 'self-consciousness' in the form of ego. The last is the transcendental, spiritual awareness, which makes the consciousness aware and makes the mind know what the knower wishes it to know through witnessing what the mind does.

It is only when we experience through consciousness that we realize any situation subjectively. Behind our illusory or relative reality lies the eternal, imperishable and limitless absolute reality of awareness, which is complete in all respects. This completeness is the Ultimate Reality. The nature of this absolute is embedded in its intelligence-energy, which manifests in the mind. Though invisible, it eternally flows from one to another, in continuum, and can neither be created nor destroyed.

It is said, that we exist in two separate selves, the perishable and the infinite. Both are a part of the same completeness. The first is identified with our ego or body-consciousness, where the self lives in duality, always dependent on something or the other. The other is our inner self, core energy, the God within us, which exists in the Absolute, being non-dual awareness. What we need to remember here is that both are constituents of the same subject — one is separated in its objectivity, while another remains intact.

In our troubled times of strife and mankind's never ending desires, it becomes all the more interesting to know what this Eastern mystical thought is all about. We remain ignorant, incomplete and inadequate due to a lack of self-knowledge, and so sadness, sorrows and suffering never leave us. Why is it that we never reach that stage, when we can confidently declare that we are content and complete, in happiness and bliss? What is this absolute existence? Does anyone reach it? What makes it so fascinating? How can it convince us about that absoluteness, or what we really are? Is there any other way by which we may ease our life, and find a solution to continually swaying into either happiness or sadness? Why can't religion or science provide a solution or an answer to this question? There are many questions, but as we read on, they all lead to one answer.

In the Western world, there is a certain lack of spiritualism, because most concepts are related to logic and the mind. The meaning of reality rests on objective existence, rather than subjective existence. Therefore, the relevance of life is expressed in the logical analysis of everything, nicely marketed, but restricted to the physical world. Therefore, the West has made tremendous progress in every factual field of science and technology, with emphasis upon physical comforts and living well. However, most westerners eventually become frustrated with life, as with this sort of reality, they become conditioned recipients, imprisoned in set formulae and assumptions, dependent largely on external factors for happiness or satisfaction. When physical wants keeps increasing, psychic problems emerge, creating emotional and psychological turbulence. This starkly underlines the need for spiritualism. In the East, spiritualism is deep-rooted and has been for thousands of years and studying the science of consciousness is as important as the science of logic and fact.

The word 'spirit' from 'spiritualism' used in this book, is to signify going beyond perceptual thoughts, into the belief that all that exists is but a manifestation of this spirit. This invisible subject, the all-pervasive cosmic energy is the source of the subject-object relationship in the form of body-mind and soul. As spirit or soul, it manifests in the mind as awareness, enlightens and forms the content of our consciousness, and enables us to be conscious of all that we perceive and conceive in the mind. We have on one extreme, ego or body consciousness, and on another, pure and total awareness. In the former, we have apparent reality, which is illusory and dual in nature and in the latter we have the Ultimate Reality as awareness. In this pure state, every aspect of existence is directed towards totality, wholeness, oneness and absoluteness. Both states are suspended as if on a weighing scale with oneness at the centre point, responsible for the development of our 'self-consciousness' to proceed towards purity.

This witnessing consciousness, also referred to as the real Self, is present in all of us, remaining indivisible and in one continuum with the all-pervasive intelligence-energy, known as *Brahman*. The truth behind this absolute reality cannot be factually, logically or intellectually explained, since this has to be felt, experienced and self-realized. Since the witnessing process through awareness isn't physical, perceptual or emotional but is experiential, it is termed by the mind and science, as being mysterious or mystical.

We all have a limited self, living for the external environment, as well as an inner Self – the mystical divine consciousness residing within. Through this 'mind of God' flows limitless awareness, which is the subject and the basis of everything. From this divine knowledge, we come to understand the reality of our presence and its Source; how matter and spirit are one and not two and the meaning of 'I am That'.

Expanding consciousness is what spiritualism is all about. The thesis being propounded has been derived from ancient philosophical scriptures written upon spiritualism. It is an attempt to illustrate the deceptions and delusions that we live in, despite all the comforts of materialism. In material reality, what we presume to be real is so hollow that it makes us depressed with life.

Even though absolute and relative as well as subjective and objective realities exist in our minds, it is the objective world of duality, which often takes precedence. It is almost as if only after you have seen the Devil, does the need for God arise. This sort of life, in which we all exist, revolves mainly around thoughts of 'I', with the support of our physical identity, forms and sensory organs.

Whereas, the inner experiential perception – depending on one's individual degree of consciousness – is free from all the constraints of the body or objectivity. It silently and subtly guides us, making us aware of another reality within, which our objective mind cannot perceive. This is the real you, your infinite inner being; not body and mind, which are bound to perish and wither. The real Self, has no name or identity. The inner self is what provides solace and serenity in this maddening and chaotic world. It is eternal, forever flowing and is meant to enlighten that being in you, which scriptures claim, exists in continuum with the Universe.

Both the external and inner selves exist and are inseparable within the mind. Both rise and reside simultaneously, as explained later. One leads to choices, conflicts, justifications and incessant wanting in ignorance; the other is sublime, free, forever flowing, silent and complete in its own Self. The need here is to embark on a journey, to integrate these aspects of our personalities and live in harmony. This is the worthy endeavour, rather than wasting our time and money in temples or on spiritual organizations. What we really need is to know how to travel in this journey of life, balancing both inner and outer needs, with a disciplined de-conditioning of our sensory mind.

God did not create heaven or hell, we invented these. We experience different degrees of heaven or hell in our own existence, depending on each individual's awareness and deeds. In fact, science now agrees, God did not create the Universe; He is very much in us, as the Creation, in every form or object we come across. Irrespective of colour, caste or creed, we need to understand and know the divine Creation within us. In this manner, we can reach out to Him, and have the best of all worlds, with the inner and outer spheres working in harmony. This book is all about understanding the divine within us, and about how to live spiritually, moment to moment, understanding and enjoying every aspect of life, without requiring assistance from any external source – religious, spiritual or psychic. The purpose of writing this book is to awaken the depths of the reality lying dormant within you.

In reality, it is very difficult to define 'who you are' because your identity is so dissolved in that universal awareness that the 'who' loses its essence. It is only for the physical self that the 'who' is important. Spiritually, it is more important to know 'what' you are. Your 'knowingness' through awareness, the reality or the source, is responsible for representing that 'who'. The degree is in being a part of that godliness when you claim 'I am That'. The 'knowingness' takes place through existential and experiential means and for this reason, 'what you are' takes centre stage. In spiritual awakening, consciousness shifts to a higher experiential level in awareness of the witnessing self, rather than your perceptual self.

Normally, we process our surroundings, through the filter of our perceptions and emotions. This makes us creatures of habit, resulting in our being only partly conscious. If we are interested in understanding the meaning of life, we need to liberate ourselves from age-old traditions and beliefs. Then we will be free to bring in fresh awareness in every facet of our existence. We will become more alive, flow more naturally, without suppressing, struggling or controlling anything. Life becomes smoother, happier and better, as long as awareness is directed in a positive manner. It is awareness that is the highest attainment of mankind. If one becomes independent of personal and emotional thoughts, beliefs and convictions, one could become more spontaneous and creative.

Conviction is a strong belief. It is an impression of the mind of what you are convinced of or has faith upon. It does not necessarily mean that you are right, just because you are convinced of a thesis as it is based upon past assumptions. It is only when you question or doubt, that your individuality emerges. You have a better chance of experiencing that doubt on your own to evidence that belief. Immediate awareness is drawn from your mind to satiate that doubt to discover the reality of what it is. The more you question, the higher will be your state of enlightenment.

The beauty of life lies in grasping, understanding and experiencing flashes of intuition by integrating them in our daily life. These flashes are trickles of awareness that one receives from the Universe to outgrow the paradoxical indulgences in our routines. Awareness is the key to liberating ourselves, bringing freshness and newness into our lives. We need not renounce or withdraw from our indulgences; we need to outgrow our weaknesses and replace them with awareness to ascend to a higher plane.

Please remember, your mind is a beautiful thinking machine. It requires navigation to steer you in the proper direction. You may navigate into positive or negative fields through awareness or stay neutral in indifference to any situation, without judgement. Use your mind to observe that mind, because it is awareness in your 'mind-consciousness', which will give you access to free will – the ability to make choices without the influence of beliefs or external factors.

Joining a spiritual organization, in my opinion, is an escapist act. You join because of ignorance, but the result is usually that you become mentally rigid and dependent, claiming that you have become free of ego, when you have not. A realized, spiritual teacher is a person who can dissolve as one with the student and impart spiritual knowledge with humility, which is not possible for an ordinary mind – the reason such teachers are so difficult to find. Any realized person, who has reached such a divine level, has very little interest in marketing and selling his knowledge through an organization or institution. He has transcended the body level and reached a place where there is only selflessness and compassion.

Ultimately, what you need to know is the truth, internally and externally. You do not need to become dependent upon listening to somebody else's experiences and realization in life; you need to experience on your own. In spiritualism, gaining self-knowledge is only the starting point; self-awareness starts one on the direction towards that core or centre, which can only be realized by existential and experiential living.

Be free and strong, do not be dictated to by any organization, person or authority; do not allow your thoughts to be influenced by any others' awareness, experience, beliefs, traditions or superstitions. To an extent, I do agree that for the weak and broken, a few such organizations may come to their rescue and act as an anchor to bring them back into life. However, if you are strong and can take care of yourself, then all you need is simple divine awareness, not from any external source, but to internally, simply existentially, rise and act.

Our mind and thoughts limit us; we do not even seem to realize our limitations, or know where to draw the line, regarding our habits, feelings and emotions. What is required of us is to know the real 'I' to decide anything. This in itself is such a spiritual gift! You have the option through your own free will to decide which divinity you will follow, a separate God or the divine in you. But for the main part we remain at sub-human level, living in a world of desires and self-pursuits, with a body and mind separated from our spirit, in transitory existence, clinging to the false imagination of our 'I'.

However, to know this 'I' from moment to moment, self-knowledge in self-awareness through self-discovery is required, where you are observing and watching yourself in complete concentration and focussing on every single thought, feeling, word and action. That is what I would call liberating oneself from the clutches of the limitations of a conditioned mind, into a pool of creativity and meditation, using the 'Mind of God'.

We are not to abandon any of our indulgences, whether in desire or luxuries, we are to observe in alertness to accept, outgrow and transform with righteousness and awareness, in a natural flow. The reason is – understanding the power of awareness in no way prohibits us from enjoying our material existence in the illusory world of comforts. This stage of materialistic worldly life is a crucial part of our existence, not to be denounced in any manner but to be accepted with grace.

Perceptions, thoughts, feelings and emotions will come and go. What remains constant however, is awareness; we are to become alert, observant, and aware to enjoy this existence of dualities. Awareness of every moment in itself will gradually upgrade our life in a natural flow, making us strong enough to outgrow and transform any negative thought, habit or attitude.

I am the happiness; I am that sadness.
I am God, and I am the Devil.
I am that presence, in awareness, of all that is there.

Chapter 4
Awareness

THE SUBJECT OF SPIRITUAL AWARENESS is generally not taken seriously, because to understand its depths or comprehend it as a cosmic energy, one needs to be well versed in Self-knowledge. Most of us justify condemning, comparing and judging others, but not ourselves. We refuse to refute the 'I' in us, being mired in feelings, beliefs and conditionings from the past, making us unaware of the reality within. Self-knowledge starts that process by which we discover our own being, in order to identify the presence of who we really are. The mind uses this sixth sense, to become aware and to be conscious of what the mind and body experience.

It is not easy to activate the mind to accept the faculty of awareness as a regular practice, especially to be fully awake to every moment of the now. We usually utilize awareness for our past experiences. However, for spiritual living, it becomes imperative to enlighten this awareness within us and go beyond our limited thoughts and beliefs from the past, into the presence of our awareness in the now.

Our actions right or wrong are taken through an individual's capacity of past and present awareness. The potential energy of the universe on manifesting in the mind becomes aware and kinetic. This awareness is not limited to time or space. Neither can this spirit be created or destroyed, or even divided into parts; it just flows in one continuum. Awareness is the subject of all of us. Being invisible, it may confuse science but it is the essence or substance of the Self. It is only through awareness that we are able to access the intricacies of the mind in its functioning.

According to the *Gita*, an ancient Indian text, there is only one, all-pervasive awareness in which all objects exist. Within this awareness, we have three types of existence. The first is perceptual, where one is submerged in sensuous pleasures and desires, bound by emotions and attachments. The second is empirical or experiential, where one uses the intellect and consciousness to live by experience and gain wisdom. The third is absolute – very rare for human beings to achieve, being reserved for those who dissolve their mind and body in selfless living with unconditional love, as achieved by Buddha and Jesus.

The mind is capable of sustaining continuous awareness, and that's what meditation is all about. Meditation is not just sitting in one corner, with your eyes closed and making an effort to shut down your mind for a few moments. That would be mental relaxation rather than meditation. Meditation is awareness that accesses your thoughts, making your mind conscious of what it thinks and indulges in. Awareness tells you much more than your thoughts, and this is what creativity and meditation is all about.

Creativity is the art of spontaneous flashes of divine intelligence merging with your mind, awakening it into a new beginning. The way any piece of art, music, painting or a poem tries to express in a subtle manner, the nature of awareness, which is a reflection from within you of serene beauty and bliss. It demands your natural purity of thought, your awareness of the now. Liberate yourself from your old thoughts, to share your intelligence in conjunction with that of the divine.

In spiritual inquiry, you will discover that apart from the materialistic world, you have another life, which is far more stable and constant, an awakened life. What is it? How do you understand and comprehend it? Is this an escapist attitude or a journey of awareness into truth and reality? As you read on, you will discover how mysterious this path is, because in this spiritual journey you cannot apply logic, only practise and experience prevail to realize the truth. You do not require any help from any outside source, to draw upon the intelligence energy of awareness.

It all begins when your mind starts to think when you are a child. Thoughts primarily commence from perceptions received from the sensory organs mainly out of the impressions of surrounding objects. In this manner, thoughts in choosing between this or that in your self-interest, culminate in desire with regards to worldly objects, filling up that empty space in your mind with thoughts of me and mine. You succumb to sensual pleasures. You begin to live a worldly life.

This goes on, until you begin to realize that even after attaining worldly objects, something is amiss. You make an effort to obtain self-knowledge and come to know the meaning of inner perceptions related to existential and experiential living. When spiritual awareness enters, you look inwards or within, beyond the extremes of right and wrong. You expand in your mind, gaining self-knowledge about the Witnessing Self, called soul or consciousness.

If you are weak, the soul remains ignorant and attaches itself to worldly objects and desires in its ego-consciousness. When you awaken from this ignorance, your spiritual personality expands and the spirit makes its real presence felt. This is the essential nature of mind that it has the capacity to experience and realize both. The spiritual journey commences through knowledge of the self, and by knowing the distinction between matter and spirit; not to culminate in ego-consciousness, but to shine with luminous awareness of divinity. Therefore, in body-consciousness, your mind, body and ego (weak and separated spirit) exhibit their prominence; however, in an awakened soul, sublime awareness reveals your true nature and reality.

Our consciousness is dependent on awareness from one moment to the next. Awareness becomes the subject of the divine spirit; and the absolute non-dual energy and consciousness, the content. Awareness remains absolute and singular, but consciousness gets to taste both non-duality and the dualities of life. The answer here is, simply be what you are; observe, be alert, listen, watch with neither feelings nor thoughts, and see how awareness embraces you. This is what real meditation is. Your moods, whims and fancies will disappear unnoticed; the deeper the watchfulness, the deeper will be your awareness.

Your mind and thoughts are now in total freedom. It may make you less efficient in the beginning, but you will definitely be more imaginative, intuitive and creative. Remember, the mind is what is known, but you, as awareness are unknown, and merging the two gives meaning to your life. Spiritual awareness in life is a creative manifestation, where nature blossoms into consciousness. This manifestation is twofold – as subject and object. One sustains the other, as the perceiver and the perceived. For this manifestation to be achievable, there exists Absolute energy, the spirit or Awareness, as the substratum of all that is in this Universe, exhibiting the Unified field of Consciousness.

The absolute manifestation of awareness in totality remains incomplete. Therefore, to attain total awareness in human existence is extremely difficult. The scriptures of Vedanta, maintained that it is ultimately the mind that knows all that it knows. The different methods of gaining epistemological knowledge as given are: perceptual, empirical and transcendental. The transcendental knowledge of awareness should never lose its identity during your normal existence in dualities. It is useful and important for us to learn, understand and allow this flow of awareness to course through us unabated, as recourse to ease the suffering within.

Today, we have the capacity to solve and satisfy innumerable physical requirements of the body and mind. However, our thought processes are still incapacitated and do not release the power of subjective awareness. In spite of every comfort and enjoyment, more of us are becoming sick with various illnesses of the mind and body. Engineering human consciousness through awareness is where the answer lies.

One should be in direct contact with one's inner being at all times. You need not go to institutes, ashrams or spiritual places for that. You will realize that you need not renounce or suppress any of your desires, as suppression may lead to confusion or magnify them. You just need to outgrow negativity with inner balance and turn away from your wrongdoings. This in itself will make you conscious, bringing in a silent change of goodness.

Your mind will automatically program itself for a new beginning, with zero resistance. You will grow out of old habits into a new awareness of what is right and wrong, and decide and navigate your thoughts the way you want. It is important not to be swayed or enamoured by the awareness or enlightenment of someone else, because this higher awareness cannot be transferred. Truth is always better felt and experienced in your own capacity as a seeker, only then can you elevate your inner world to rise in divinity.

Thoughts are often trapped in the framework of your mind to think only about 'I, me and mine'. It is in that silence, deep within yourself from your own mind, that the unadulterated manifestation of energy called awareness, ignites. It is responsible for turning your thoughts into that perceptive content called consciousness. This pure awareness being invisible, is mysterious, cannot be inferred by thoughts and is non-dual in nature. The more we discover, thoughts become better, rational and more neutral. We may receive this awareness in spontaneous flashes or through a disciplined effort of the mind. This awareness in me, truly defines 'who I am', because the higher the characteristic of non-dual awareness, the higher and closer we are to the divine within us.

Awareness is considered by many to be mystical, as there is no explanation of its source. When we say, "I am that awareness", and agree that we are all part of the same energy, then it may be safe to presume that this uncorrupted awareness-energy flows from the same eternal source. Furthermore, awareness on its own has no role to play. Raw energy turns into awareness-intelligence only upon manifesting in the mind. The higher the level of awareness, the more the content in consciousness, and the more peaceful and happier we are.

Therefore, just by knowing the divine presence within you or 'I am that divine awareness' is not enough. The only way would be to build an attitude where you are convinced that existing in dualities, forms illusions in your mind, and that you need to transcend such everyday attitudes to reach towards that absoluteness, in order to accept yourself and behave neutrally in both happiness and sorrow. When you build such an attitude and start living with observation and alertness to accept all in awareness, negative factors will automatically depart from your life. Once you become aware through the power of observation, watching carefully when you habitually indulge in your vices, say in smoking, alcoholism, multiple sex, cheating, etc., you will outgrow what you do not approve of without having the need to force yourself.

We become players in this game of life and death, with our hungry senses playing the game of dividing and demarcating everything and anything into 'mine' or 'yours.' Thoughts, emotions and ideas upon everything are divided for the sake of body-mind comfort. More important than this is who we are and what we wish to become. Awareness decides these things, and in awareness every single thought and perception becomes important. We are what we are, at the level of our awareness. In an unfinished stage we are mortal but in Total Awareness we are complete and immortal.

In this book of expressing my thoughts, while living in the same illusory, dual life, as all of us, the best I can say is, enjoy every moment of life to its fullest, but be in spontaneous awareness. Right or wrong, or what limits one needs to set, should be decided freely within your own awareness, with the help of your own spiritual consciousness. Just as no medicine can have the same effect on everyone, in the same manner no master, institution or authority can transfer awareness to you that is specific to your requirements. All you need is to be mentally strong and disciplined; you need not go to anybody to take charge of your inner life.

When you are young, you are innocent, confident and positive; you do not require any guru or external support. For that matter, you don't even think of God, unless compelled by elders. As you age, your mind becomes constricted and conditioned by others. Living in the past, in anxiety and fear, dividing into this and that, we start seeking refuge from the outside.

Fear remains deep within, disturbing the rhythm of our life. You may require a master, mainly for this reason, but only as a guide to show you the general direction. Otherwise he will take away your personal freedom and power from you. In the Self, you are your own master, with freedom and awareness as your own personal power, which will determine the strength and character of your individuality.

Life is a mystery; the only way to unravel it is through awareness. The best part of obtaining awareness is that nothing in life should be suppressed, opposed, or struggled against. It just requires you to open your eyes and keep looking and watching in the right manner. You indulge, outgrow and transform gradually, whether towards the positive or negative, but with awareness. This way we can evolve without any resistance and in total acceptance, and automatically drop what we do not require, without anyone telling us what to do or not to do.

As mentioned earlier, there is nothing in awareness that needs to be preached or for any master to share his experiences with others. Awareness comes from impulse, either naturally or by being disciplined. Therefore, we need not shun, become overwhelmed by or negate desire; we are to accept, enjoy and allow it to dissolve and mature within us with awareness. A human brain functions in its thought patterns. These patterns are formed in impressions created by perceptions in their respective interpretations of our daily life – making our reality. These thoughts settle into our subconscious as memory. One function of the subconscious, out of many, is to store all the thoughts and experiences of our life, summing up to form our consciousness.

Consciousness reflects the deeper reality within, from our past and our self-oriented beliefs, working on autopilot, exhibiting itself when required by our conditioned mind (e.g. after we have consciously learned how to walk or swim, these actions get embedded into our subconscious, so we need not learn them again). The subconscious plays a very important role in how we condition our minds. In fact, we are what our subconscious or conditioned mind dictates. This becomes the truth of our life, explaining many experiences of the past and anxious concerns for the future. The subconscious needs constant awareness of the now, either to awaken, upgrade or alter old habits. Yes, our old, habitual thoughts were once new, but many a times, they need overhauling with awareness for our betterment.

When it flows naturally, awareness that springs from the subconscious is at times superior to that attained by spontaneity or discipline. Utilizing awareness in such cases, moment to moment, becomes a natural or automatic effort, rather than an exercise. This may be the reason why we come across some people, who are naturally self-controlled and realized, not having to make much effort to achieve such an evolved state. They are aware of the now, by the nature and character of their own subconscious, simply by habit.

As awareness dawns, you gradually outgrow your weaknesses and begin feeling different. You move with the flow of existence, like a river; you do not become disturbed or nervous easily. You brush off the old thoughts that keep coming back to deplete your energy. Conflicts are reduced, you do not resent, regret or even judge anyone. You start becoming a witness to all that is happening around. You walk, sit and eat with awareness. You enjoy every moment of your life. You no longer consider anyone your enemy. In fact, you try and make a positive effort to be more understanding, appreciating people as they are. You criticize less and make fewer comments about others. You feel the calm of emptiness; your drive towards materialistic growth is reduced. You change; you no longer want to spend hours with friends with whom you indulge in nothing but petty talk. You seem to become a stranger to them. You have more silence in your life than ever before.

This silence, you realize, communicates better with awareness than it used to, and you did not force anything onto yourself. You just went with the flow, and a gradual transformation took place. You are no longer disturbed and lonely; you can enjoy your own company in solitude. You have become more conscious of existence itself and your mind no longer chatters about its own egoistic thoughts. Now, you wish to reach a stage in which absolutely nothing can shake your equilibrium and sense of peace. Good, bad or ugly, to you they should all be the same – a part of the same completeness, emptiness or oneness to which we all belong.

This has been my own experience. After imbibing the depth behind awareness as well as its significance, you need not regulate, suppress or resist anything, or any desire. You naturally develop a habit, through your subconscious, to always be aware as an astute observer. For you, God and the Devil become but two sides of the same coin — you no longer need to choose. Your subconscious takes the necessary decisions and ensures you act both for your benefit and in oneness with all, maintaining the right balance.

You might wonder why am I going to such lengths to elaborate upon the effect of awareness, repeatedly and the effect it has on each one of us? The reason is, awareness is the subject of us all, and this book. It may just be one word out of many in our dictionary and it may seem to be simple to understand in its meaning, but to really understand its spiritual ramifications, that awareness is the presence of 'who we are', is a much more complex endeavour. It can take time to get to know its magic, what it can do for you and to understand its real depths. It has taken me over ten years to be able to jot down all that you can read in these books. After understanding the essence of awareness, the rest becomes easy and natural, as you practice, day-by-day, moment-to-moment.

This begs the question, why is awareness, the subject of our consciousness, the ultimate core energy, eternal and limitless, so very important to the meaning of our lives? Why is it that the same importance has not been expressed by various masters on this subject? The answer is simple. Like the billion dollar pharmaceutical industry or its practitioners will not strongly emphasize eating, sleeping, exercising and thinking well, as the ultimate answer to health, very few gurus will go this deep, and convey that ultimately we are nothing but energy in awareness.

Our body and mind decompose back into energy after our death, it is only our consciousness comprising of our awareness, which remains to join the grid of universal consciousness. When we depart from this existence, our body-mind may no longer be there, but the journey of life continues. Our thoughts in words and actions remain etched in the future. We give or receive from the energy of unified consciousness every moment. However, our identity remains, our uniqueness carries on with our own signature in the manner it may remain in this book that I am writing. We have the ability to shape our future after our body decays in the continuation of its soul. At the same time, I cannot give all the credit to the future, as my identity is being revealed in my actions in the now, making it a cause of determining my future. Every thought we emit bears our identity, remaining forever. We are an extension of our parents and will be in continuation through our children.

It is purely a continuation of one form of energy into another; we come from dust and go back into the same dust. It is only through understanding this continuation that we can make our identity worthy and beautiful through our thoughts, words and actions. This continuation need not wait for birth or death, it simply continues from one form of energy into another. Therefore, awareness is the ultimate answer to mental health. It has to be experienced and realized without help from any master, and that is the mantra, which can enhance individuality, uniqueness or consciousness. Success belongs only to those who are spontaneous in the now. This brings in the required freshness in how they think and act. Those who follow and believe blindly in the knowledge and awareness gained by others can only talk and argue, but not act and succeed.

I repeat, no guru, master or preacher can increase your level of awareness for you. It is a purely existential process, where the intelligence-energy, present in you, manifests in accordance to your demands. You become so free and so strong, you can rise above any former blind faith in a religion, spiritual centres or any association. As you are now aware, you will realize such cures are like that of any psychiatrist, addressing only the periphery of the real issues. All their pomp and show is to project themselves as messiahs or messengers of God. They do help, but like a painkiller does, curing your headache only temporarily.

Received 'wisdom' tells us that God and the Devil are both within us; it is for us to become aware and conscious about them. They also tell us that the vices, which restrict humility and bring down positive energies are: arrogance, anger, greed, jealousy, obsession and lust. What you are required to do is become honest, be truthful and accept the presence of any of these within you. If you ask me, I have all six, but by being constantly aware, as and when they appear, I am gradually outgrowing such indulgences without much effort. I further try to replace the above negatives with habits of positivity like: giving, truth, love, faith and detachment. I wish the same for all of you.

In science, truth is that inference
in its theory of Reductionism.
In philosophy, truth is what it constantly seeks.
In spiritualism, truth is an experience
of now in absoluteness.

Chapter 5
What is Truth?

The truth is simple and eternal; it does not change with time and space. It is an experience of the now, which can only be felt; it changes the moment your thoughts try to describe it in words. Truth simply exists and is beyond belief, faith and hope. It exists irrespective of whether anyone believes it or not. Philosophers, scientists, wise men utilize the methods of logic, scientific inference and reasoning to declare that something they think is true. However, with new discoveries, the 'truth' keeps changing within a given space and time. What was termed true later turns out to be false and the 'truth' starts differing. Hence, the absolute truth is highly elusive, especially when it relates to the world of objects.

Truth, in spiritual terms is pure existence, the subject of everything in the emptiness of our Universe. The presence of your being in the now is the truth, a part of the whole. It cannot be explained in words or language; it is an experience that you feel and then realize. In the objective world, truth is related to untruth and is limited to time and space. This is pure duality and therefore, an illusion. What is considered as 'truth' here is apparent and impermanent. In this relativistic world, where energy changes its form from matter back to energy and vice versa but in itself remains constant, it signifies that the basic constituent of energy is the truth and the Ultimate Reality.

In the quest for the truth about oneself, one realizes that body and mind are only transitory mass or matter, and prone to decompose into its subject: energy. It is only awareness, the constructs of consciousness, which reveals the truth that we are a part of the subject and not the object, which the mind presumes us to be.

Recently, I read a quote, which said, "The tragedy of modern man is not that he knows less and less about the truth of his own life, but that it bothers him less and less." The truth is that most of us do not understand the inner conflict within us, neither do we bother to know ourselves truthfully. We are too occupied in judging others to accurately judge our own self. If we do not even know the truth within us, how can we come to know the truth of reality and the Universe?

We travel from thought to thought, turning them into ideas and concepts, grouping them, bundling them, brooding over them, but in any situation, they are associated with past knowledge. We also hold on to these self-same thoughts well into the future, as they are dictated by memory, or by our prejudiced feelings and emotions telling us what to think and do.

Reality and truth are the same — they exist eternally. The thoughts, which our knowledge is based upon, are primarily dependent on our past. This way, we become imprisoned in our 'me' and 'mine' forming our ego, providing a personal identity based mainly on emotions, living in a world of our own likes and dislikes, emotions and memories; limiting ourselves, and turning the same old thoughts into beliefs.

Life is far bigger than mere beliefs or a faith based upon the past. If we really wish to liberate ourselves, become free, and know our truth, we have to allow the mind to penetrate deeper into the reality of the now. Stop clinging to the past. We need to go beyond our thought processes, beliefs, traditions, illusions, apparent reality, and our choices as these create conflicts and lead us to become victimized. What you accept as true, may just be an opinion or what any doctrine declares, a belief; these are not necessarily the truth, in the real sense of the word or concept.

Therefore, when we choose between this and that, know that the mechanism of choice is only an instinct drawn from past thoughts. These thoughts are constructed mainly based upon responses and reactions to any situation connected with the past. The mind reacts from past knowledge to counter any situation. For e.g. in danger, the mind reacts out of fear, whereas in physical love, the mind reacts out of attraction.

There will be no newness, freshness, uniqueness or freedom in our minds besides our 'I, me, mine and myself', dancing in past glory, unless we are proactive instead of being reactive. This will require the presence of the now, grabbing the space between our thoughts, before our minds can intervene to opine, judge and act in self-interest.

Until we get out of the ambit of the small 'I' and its limited egoistic thoughts, the mind cannot manifest pure, creative intuitiveness. Only after attaining knowledge of the self does the divine 'I' start to grow. We become conscious, more awareness enters and filters through our mind, expanding our intellect. This allows us to learn the truth and the eternal presence of who we really are – which lies beyond emotional ego-consciousness.

We keep hearing or reading about the power of thought, the super-human results that thoughts can achieve, where you just need to demand and command, and it shall be given. Of course, if it were that easy, most of us would have been super-human. Yes, thoughts do play a significant role in programming and interpreting what the mind wishes by creating wonders in the materialistic world. Spiritually, however, it is just the opposite — the less you think, the better it is. Thus, you can fine-tune your awareness to become responsive in creativity.

Thoughts of external perception have less meaning; they take too much time and tend to act via the mind in choosing and reacting only in self-interest, creating conflicts. It is the inner perception of spontaneous awareness that provides real fuel to the brain. The pure, fresh creative energy of immediate awareness makes the mind come alive, boosting creativity and intuitiveness.

This awareness is your big 'I', which is responsible for making you think. Awareness is primary; it manifests prior to consciousness and perception. Awareness being the primary subject of this book, it is explained in detail practically in every chapter. Awareness has no link or identification with anything; it is changeless, choice-less, timeless, limitless, absolute energy. Awareness of the now is the subject and presence of who we are. It refers to the eternal, non-dual intelligence-energy manifesting in the mind.

When it relates to the past or logical awareness, it is connected to self-consciousness in thoughts.

When you find yourself beset by anger, envy or jealousy, detach yourself from the situation and simply watch the mind playing its chattering game by luring you into negative emotions. Watching and observing will bring that required awareness where you will introspect and contemplate if it is really worth wasting all that energy, consuming negative thoughts of jealousy, hatred, etc. You then transform your mental *modus operandi* to observing your mind instead of analysing in self-interest and so transcend from petty thoughts into acceptance of reality in grace.

Absolute reality, meaning total awareness, or pure consciousness has not been given much significance in science, which can neither perceive nor conceive of the meaning behind this invisible radiant energy. The answer to this mystery lies in the fact that the energy that is liberated and is not bound by space and time is what is referred to as the Absolute Truth or Total Awareness.

Truth is objective in its relativity, like a picture frame is true and real as long as it exists; tear the picture and break the frame and see how both disappear. Truth or reality in its absolute form is changeless and limitless; it cannot be limited or dictated by cults, religions or society. It cannot be imposed or conditioned by belief and tradition, which is a common phenomenon today.

In reality, you are constantly influenced from the time of your birth until your death. Your mind is blocked and conditioned to such an extent, that you are more a product of others – parents, teachers, preachers, etc. – rather than your own. From your name, your religion, to your education, others dictate significant areas of your life. This alters your personality or individuality, making you dependent and always requiring guidance in whatever you think and do. Such a situation also takes you away from your own truth.

How can you relate to the truth, when you are being either victimized by others or dependent on others through attachments and desires in your own mind? Here truth becomes subjugated to your mental bondages. In following others' regimes and dictates, you are taken away from your free inner self, leaving your mind to become rigid and opaque to the truth.

Those who really wish to be free, without any conditioning, from childhood or otherwise, display more energy and intensity. They have an ever-growing desire to remove all attachments and they make an effort to understand the meaning of life truthfully and in totality, rather than in spurts of duality. They require proof for every blind belief.

In religion, the 'truth' can never be questioned; this truth is dependent on faith and beliefs and anything inexplicable is considered a manifestation of the supernatural. Because of blind faith and various mental blocks, people with vested interests take advantage of such sentiments throughout the world and utilize this weakness for their benefit. This is the reason we see so much death in the name of religion.

The truth, in relative mode or in the dualities of existence, has a different meaning. Even though the absolute truth is unchangeable, here it differs with each person. Under the scientific method, we see a lot of data and facts being collected to obtain the truth, but again those are prone to change in due course. The truth, in such cases, is erratic; it is clouded with thoughts and emotions. It seems that truth, in our relative life, was born only after someone was caught lying.

The problem is the mind always moves into the future but functions by depending on its past, whereas the truth resides only in the present, in the here and now. So the truth, which the mind seems to or tries to perceive, is only apparent, temporary, or ephemeral. The truth and the mind seldom meet. The truth is being in the present, it has to be felt and experienced; you cannot keep chasing it, you have to discover it.

I once read somewhere, that for a man, a woman is an object of desire, to a hermit a distraction and for a tiger, a good meal. As this proves, truth cannot be apprehended in a relative manner; it differs from one to another. Absolute truth, which is changeless, timeless and limitless can only be experienced and realized.

Religion claims that we are a creation of God.
Science claims creation in the form of random collisions in particles of energy.
Spiritualism claims that the creator is the creation itself.

Chapter 6
Science, Religion and Spirituality

Science is accustomed to evolutions and revolutions. It constantly changes and corrects itself; it is open to any belief and these are researched and corrected repeatedly to improve the overall body of scientific knowledge. In just two decades, room-sized computers have been transformed into handheld ones in the form of tablets and mobile phones.

Religion on the other hand is still dependent on faith and beliefs. There is no movement to improve upon its testaments and rituals. Perhaps, if like science, it is able to accept the realities of life, there may be a chance for religion to become a greater force. Sadly, in these times, religion is reliant upon politics and economics and even tries to snatch spiritualism within its ambit. However, somehow, even today, mainly due to the strong sense of separatism engendered by it, which results in ego – religion imposes its superiority over both science and spiritualism.

I happened to come across an article about a renowned award-winning scientist in the US, Raymond Kurzweil, who works in the field of reverse engineering of aging and death via artificial intelligence. According to him, by the year 2045, the phenomenon of the singularity will be real. There would be hundreds of microchips implanted in our body and mind, reducing the difference between humans and machines. We would become a hybrid of biological and non-biological intelligence. He also claims that computers may control our consciousness as well. If this turns out to be real, the achievement of the singularity may bring an end to the human era.

With technology zipping ahead at such a pace, the abstract mind is bound to give in to the 'super' mind.

However, as of now, man's most probable future shows only an increase in decay, suffering, and mental imbalance with an unconscious, self-centred mind finding no peace. In fact, it seems to be degenerating into a sub-human mind. How the future will unfold and whether technology or artificial intelligence will win over human intelligence, is still a big question. However, when it comes to self-actualization, it has become imperative that humans embrace both worldly and spiritual life – whether we call it mysticism or spirituality – in order to find peace and fulfilment.

Traditional spiritual methods and values are in fact more relevant today than they would have been during ancient times. They are to be integrated into our worldly life, to balance our incessant desires and attachments and facilitate self-analysis with self-awareness to accept the imperfections we need to transform and outgrow. For this to happen, there is no need for us to become monks, chant mantras the whole day or visit ashrams to attain spiritual enlightenment. Spirituality simply revolves around existential and experiential living to realize awareness in self-knowledge.

There should be a fusion of science and spiritualism in the world – science, to tackle the world of objects, and spiritualism, to elaborate upon the subject of life, giving science a fillip to evolve further. Religion on the other hand, is nothing but an offshoot of spiritualism in reality. In the higher realms, both religion and spiritualism merge into one. In the current situation, both religion and spiritualism have been gradually poisoned for the sake of money, power and fame. The intention might be to keep followers entrapped, dependent, and rigid; to be influenced and utilized as and when such advisors feel like it, in blindness, with no awareness.

Buddha, Jesus and many others like them did not belong to any religion when they were revealing their awareness through unconditional love for everyone. Their teachings have been distorted, creating a separate God, institutions and a set of caste, culture, and creeds, as is the case for most religions.

Science has mastered the outer world, making great progress in understanding the physical and the visible. Morality and consciousness, however, are not subjects with which science is too comfortable. Moreover, science has not been able to explain how neural activity can give rise to what we characterize as experience or even what spiritualism refers to as the Witnessing Self in the form of consciousness. The only reliable means science has of reaching an agreement on these subtle aspects of reality is the fact that scientists too have a consciousness or that even they can observe and perceive consciousness experientially in another conscious being.

In the worldly domain, an individual perceives life materialistically, relating to it through ego and vanity. Whether negative or positive, religious or atheist, moneyed or intellectual, each one of us wants to show his superiority over another. In this manner, we cling to our attachments and ego in fear and insecurity, wanting more and more. We are more concerned about what others think of us, than in knowing our own self. This is where spiritualism comes in to counter materialistic life with the message of inner balance, starting with self-knowledge, self-awareness, and self-realization. However, spiritualism, if not followed properly, can encourage an escapist attitude and become a crutch for the mentally weak to lean on and inflate a hollow ego.

Science is for worldly objects and materialism, separating everything that it can perceive into parts. Spiritualism is just the opposite; its basic message is: all that exists is but a manifestation of One. For science, thoughts of perception are everything; spiritualism demands a no-mind zone, where thoughts should not be present.

In the world of materialism, consciousness merges with ego; in spiritualism, it merges in purity towards the one and only divine. In between, we have awareness, constructing our consciousness and leaning towards either materialism or divinity. Our intellect, through the personal power of individuality, determines the outcome.

Spiritual life should in no way be separate from daily life. Neither should you shun or negate ego. The only method which will silence the mind and make it turn towards divinity, is knowledge and awareness in observance and acceptance of ego. After all, our mind is all that we have and in which existence is a self-contained entity. Perceiving and observing the self is also the only reality we can conceive. Therefore, how we use our mind to ferry us through life forms the essence of our individuality.

In some ways, religion seems to be lost in its own glory — championing its own beliefs, traditions and faith, taking even spiritualism into its own ambit. However, spiritualism makes its precepts very clear by declaring that God, Guru, and Self are all within you.

Apart from the factors of science, religion, and spirituality, we have another factor – money, which plays a significant role in our life. British media recently reported upon data collected from 126 countries, that a majority of respondents felt that happiness is dependent on wealth earned and used in a righteous manner. I would say, even for peace of mind, at any stage of life, one needs an ample amount of money, if not huge amounts. Like the mind, money is a great tool if used properly, but if both are victimized under the influence of either; it can be highly detrimental to our existence. If money has indeed become the primary requisite to satiate mind and body, spiritual living is the answer to settle the restlessness of the modern hyperactive mind, which arises due to materialism.

Spiritual living, as explained earlier, should not have any link to associations or centres. Living, best experiences it with spontaneous awareness from one moment to the next and in being true to one's own self. Living meditatively to fulfil our wants, without suppressing our desires, with awareness, in balance and moderation is the aim of a realized life.

The key to the completeness or oneness of mind, body and beyond lies in spiritualism. The higher the degree of spiritual living, higher will be the sense of totality. Spiritual living shows you the path of how to indulge, outgrow, and transform, to bring yourself out of incessant desires and manifest in love and divinity. It provides you that inner balance and strength you need, to counter the intoxicating effects of materialism. No religion or externalized discourse can provide such grace, or be in such communion with that God within you.

Through the perceptual power of the human mind, science has progressed from bicycles to spaceships, from bows and arrows to missiles, from the cloning of living creatures to defying or delaying physical death. Human consciousness has not been addressed though; amidst all his comforts and luxuries, man remains imprisoned in his own illusions about life, without understanding the reality and purpose of his existence. For this reason, life remains incomplete, notwithstanding all the opulence and plenitude in the world.

Religion, on the other hand, has been left far behind with its old traditions and superstitions. It has degenerated into politics, power, and war. It remains conceptually stagnant, except for what it keeps borrowing from spiritualism. Its main function seems to be a rigid form of identification nowadays, only to prove that we are of this or that religion.

Spiritualism explains that cosmic energy on manifesting in the mind turns into awareness, making your mind aware to be conscious of how mind and body function both internally and in relation to the outside world. Awareness enters the mind as fresh, uncorrupted energy and because of its sheer spontaneous presence in our mind, it stimulates our knowledge through creativity and intuitiveness before our thoughts can interfere.

The higher the levels of this pure energy, the stronger our awakening and the better we are at countering negative factors lurking deep within our illusory vision of life. The second source of psychic energy is the information received through the sense organs as perceptions. This form of energy when interpreted via thoughts is limited to objects with a defined purpose – to fulfil our desires.

Alternatively, the energy manifesting in the mind awakens us and we are told to seek our own truth and reality. Through this awareness, each one of us, at some time or the other, during times of distress, contemplation or introspection, wonder about how victimized we are. In the objective world of thoughts, feelings and emotions, there arises a time, when we feel the need to become aware of a higher path in life.

Albert Einstein explained that matter and energy are the same and are interchangeable. Meaning, a beam of light and say an almond, are the same. That is, we are all composed of energy – in gross, subtle and core dimensions. Energy can neither be created nor destroyed; we can be conceptualized as a form of condensed energy in slow vibration and we go back into formless energy. Objects may seem solid or disjointed, depending on their density, frequency of wavelengths and vibrations, but are always in a continuum.

Stephen Hawking, a renowned physicist and academic celebrity, argues that God never created the Universe. According to him, because of the laws of nature such as gravity, the Universe can and will create itself from nothing. So let us go further to discover how spiritualism is the need of the hour if we wish to stabilize our lives. Although this book is based on an ancient Eastern philosophy, dating back five thousand years, you will realize how germane it is even today in our day-to-day lives.

In self-knowledge, you know of the spirit.
In self-awareness, you are conscious of the spirit.
In self-experience, you taste that spirit.
In self-consciousness, you enjoy the spirit in dualities.
In self-realization, you become one with the spirit.

Chapter 7
Knowledge of the Self

Life is like a coin — on one side we are told of that Witnessing Self, in the form of pure consciousness, which is eternal and on the other, we have an impression that our possessions and attachments towards family and wealth will remain forever. However, when death approaches, the real meaning of life dawns, revealing how ephemeral the relationship of our body and mind is to wealth and attachments.

If the same coin remains balanced and straight, without flipping to either side, it would describe the ideal role constant awareness plays in our lives. Spontaneous awareness lies beyond knowledge or impressions gained through perception. Besides, whatever knowledge one may have gained, one remains ignorant, unless such knowledge is experienced. The knowledge that I am sharing is about understanding the meaning of how to indulge in alertness with observation, acceptance, experience, and realization, towards that Absolute in awareness. This is the fundamental process of spiritualism.

Accept and meditate, from moment to moment, in the here and now. Make it a routine in daily life, fusing knowledge or intellect with awareness. This is what spirituality should be. It subtly draws you away from the usual chattering of your mind, bringing in fresh energy, rather than allowing you to brood over the past. External knowledge lies in the pursuit of the comforts of the body and mind only. We remain ignorant about that absoluteness or completeness of our inner Witnessing Self, being so deeply engrossed in the dualities of our existence that we continue to live in sorrow and suffering.

It is the job of science to prove how the cognizor splits intelligence energy into cognition of the cognized object. The intention of our study is to go beyond and discover that ingredient which awakens empirical knowledge in us through that Witnessing Self, providing not illusions but pure transcendental knowledge. The knowledge of this Self clarifies who, what and how you are in the process of bringing the subject-object closer towards oneness, from the relative to the absolute.

In sense perceptions, the mind separates the subject from its object; body and mind act in self-interest and desires. Even in inner perception through experiences, the mind indulges in 'self-consciousness' to thrive on ego and arrogance. It is only in the final release from the mind, through awareness in continued meditation that the real Self unites. Then what remains is the non-dual Supreme Self.

Knowledge of the Self is related to the understanding of the question: "Who are you?" In objective, worldly life, this 'who' plays an important role in defining the separated individual body and mind with varied identifications. Spiritually, the experiencer in the body and mind consumes and generates energy to transcend and realize the true nature of Ultimate Reality. This reality is concerned more with 'what you are' rather than 'who you are'.

Without the mind, the experiencer has no other reliable means of knowing the source of his core and the source of his life, which is so crucial to his existence. A subject-object relationship is thereby created, wherein because existence entails physicality, the material world becomes equally important in representing the totality of creation. The knowledge of the Self reveals the fact that our body is transitory by first eliminating the illusory and perceptual 'who you are', bringing in the presence of 'what you are'. This transcendence of the experiencer from ego-self to the presence of the Self is the essence of ultimate knowledge.

The knowledge of the Self also reveals the perfection of the Universe. Even God is replaced by the all-pervading and all-pervasive presence of awareness, forming the context rather than the content of 'who' we are. The final stage in self-realization is realized when this context becomes pure, pristine and non-dual, where body, mind and soul become one. Then there is no 'thinkingness', no images, impressions or memories. Pure consciousness takes the place of awareness.

The luminance that reveals all objects and establishes the foundation of all knowledge is beyond the purview of the subject-object relation; there is no dependency on anything. Therefore, what we are is the effulgence of awareness in that presence, and the presence is nothing but spirit or energy, manifesting in the mind to become aware. What remains eternally is not existence but 'life'. What remains finally is the divinity of that source, which is realized only by surrendering the ego to selflessness, compassion, and fearlessness to discover the final stage of life.

Therefore, knowledge of the self does not relate to the object of body and mind, which is the role of science. It goes beyond understanding into the core of the inner self – that Witnessing Self, the realm of the subject – probing what we really are. This knowledge, being so complex, needs to be derived by somebody who is self-realized or who has mastered the subject of spirituality. The self pertains to that Witnessing Self within your body, called pure consciousness, which guides your perceptive mind, and is the real 'you'. Here, you need to remember that in pure consciousness, you are in parity with total awareness in becoming One.

It is awareness, which ignites consciousness into purity and it is your external perception, which brings it into duality. Between the two, lies the personal power of reasoning, that deciding factor called individuality. Awareness is non-dual absolute energy, which lies beyond mind, body, and consciousness. It is the source and existed prior to everything else.

The cycle of psychic energy starts with spontaneous awareness, developing into intuition, imagination, or fresh creativity in the form of an idea. This further merges with thoughts from the subconscious, and joins with intellect, to determine your intentions. It reveals your power of reasoning and individuality, informing your intention to indulge and experience, transferring that data to your subconscious, and forming memory or past awareness.

All this tells us that there has to be a being or the presence of some substance, observing your mind, becoming that 'rememberer' and controlling your subconscious — who is forever present in all three states: awake, dream, and deep sleep. One who remains a distant observer but is not affected by the states of the mind. It also shows us that the 'rememberer' and experiencer cannot be different but are the same, clarifying the concept of 'who' you really are.

In this process, through the cumulative series of experiences, which one consciously goes through in existence, the 'rememberer' is deemed to reside in the subconscious, which is the storehouse of memory in the mind. Consciousness or the 'rememberer' in its purity is referred to as the Witnessing Self. It subtly guides our perpetual thoughts to gain new experiences. However, when attached to an object, this consciousness experiences the experience of dualities in separation and is then said to be in 'self-consciousness'.

Since knowledge can never provide total freedom, being restricted to mind, body and objects, it provides us more reason to go beyond, into spiritual living, towards absolute reality. The closer we get to this reality, the less the duality and confusion. It is only in spiritual awareness that we go deeper, where we interconnect and interrelate all that exists in the Universe.

Both the objective and the subjective world become less dependent on the mind and more on observation in awareness. There is more 'knowingness' and love. Gradually, this reduces jealousy, condemnation, judgment, and justifications, translating into compassion, drawing us closer to the totality, reality or creation to which we all belong. This makes possible a fusion of worldly life with spiritual living, and superficial reality with deeper reality — inspiring us to rise with the growth of our consciousness.

Thoughts mean everything to us. For instance, I couldn't have written a single word without my thoughts to guide me. Body, mind and thoughts are all what we have and they are the reason we exist. It is the temple in which God dwells. The need to transcend arises when the conflicts within us move towards anxiety, despair and suffering. To achieve self-actualization, it is the understanding and practice of spiritualism, which is paramount. Between worldly and spiritual living, it is awareness, which acts as the axis that tilts the balance towards peace and fulfilment.

This is an area where Buddha's philosophy is of even greater value. His conception of the four noble truths – the elevated states of mind, which is possible because of meditation – is the conduit to awakening. He discovered 'the middle path' a way of moderation and balance between two extremes. He realized after years of fasting, becoming weakened and starved, that self-denial, self-mortification and abstinence do not work.

In theory, yes, we definitely need to know about asceticism, but in normal living, we need both materialistic and spiritual dimensions. Every individual is required to inquire into his own truth or he remains a wanderer bound between love and hatred. Compassion and love for righteous living demands that your love should possess such purity of absoluteness, that it should touch even your enemy. Even though this approach may not be easy, the Buddha's basic teachings do guide us about how to raise the quality of our lives, bringing moderation and balance to reduce the misery and selfishness, which emerge out of ego.

How can one live a sane life without being true or honest to one's own self? When judging ourselves, how many of us are honest, free and detached from personal feelings and thoughts? Alternatively, are we aware of how our thoughts influence what we think and feel, moment-to-moment, day-to-day, every day? Aren't we lost, confused and disturbed most of the time?

On the path of self-knowledge or knowing that inner self, one should learn how to be honest by practicing zero self-judgment. We are generally not true to our own selves, because of our habit of justifying this or that. Whatever our egoist mind tells us, that becomes our truth. This is the reason we have so many differences and arguments, with the mind always trying to judge others and defending one's own acts and opinions, which may not be correct sometimes.

To be in the now, beyond thoughts of perception, to act individually, with no help from an external source and being honest with yourself – are the first steps to elevate yourself. You need to watch and observe your thoughts in silence for spiritual awareness to percolate. The more you know yourself, the higher your level of self-development. Only then, can you discover and expand your consciousness.

You will notice that besides your perceptual-self, there is always something telling you how far and to what extent you may indulge in any situation. To know this Witnessing Self, which runs parallel to your thoughts of perception, you need to first free yourself of your normal thoughts as they are prone to be biased to protect you in self-interest, irrespective of right or wrong. Secondly, know that what you think is mainly based on the past. These thoughts can twist and turn any situation to suit the ego's convenience.

I repeat, start to observe in the spontaneity of the now, without taking refuge in your thoughts; be alert and observant, and witness how and what your mind thinks. Further, be aware and watchful; become choiceless, allowing that inner self to talk to you. You will be able to see and feel the difference. Contemplate who you really are. You will realize how easy it was to judge others earlier, as compared to being true and knowing your own self.

The body is continually changing while the mind moves in the sphere of the known. For most of us, the mind is ruled by emotions and controlled by desires and urges. The real test of life lies in constantly challenging the mind, in order to use the mind and not be used by it, through emotional outbursts.

This is the secret to self-development, experiencing on your own; not dictated by spiritual discourses. Those who are alight with life, enrich their intellect with such new awareness all the time. They keep away from the paths laid down by cults, creeds, institutions or religions. They remain in a state of alert readiness to learn something new, become aware of the totality of existence and stay in balance. Institutions cannot make man spiritual; they only create further weakness – a bondage thriving on egotism. What we need is inner freedom, in order to practice the basics of spirituality, not through others' experiences but our own awareness of one moment to the next.

All the perceptual data from the sensory organs in your mind, after analysis, are directed only towards self-interest. You see, feel, hear, smell and taste what your mind tells you. The mind is designed for desires and attachments, which leads to conflicts. Alternatively, when you start on the journey to understand life beyond perceptions – awareness, observation, truth, self-knowledge, watchfulness etc., all become necessary.

A time comes when there is no judgment or justification. You simply allow situations to happen, observing and accepting them as they open a new world of meaning and understanding.

Understanding the difference between the two extremes — ego-consciousness and pure consciousness — is essential to understand the real meaning of life.

In ego-consciousness, we are limited to the personal self. Happiness and sadness exist in relativity. Our actions are done and credited to our 'I'. In such a state, life remains a vicious cycle of pleasure and pain. In this stage, you need to either liberate or balance them, to understand the bondage of duality. Understand how your limited consciousness of the body-mind relationship becomes the cause of your ignorance.

Spiritualism says that we come from nothing and dissolve back into nothing; we are but a manifestation of a single spirit or energy in continuum. How does the growth of body and mind become directly proportionate to your degree of self-awareness? Let us go further and see how one can understand this energy.

The knowledge of the self also involves psychoanalysis; as you may wish to understand yourself better to achieve maximum effectiveness. In our case, this energy is applied to the study of the spirit and related to what this ancient philosophy is trying to tell us. Spirituality states that on performing self-inquiry, one learns that we are, all interconnected and interrelated, a part of a single energy. Once this oneness of energy or *Brahman* is separated, existence in opposites or dualities commences.

The subject is separated into objects, and existence starts to discern and discriminate to fulfil desires. Even though life in dualities is a part of the same oneness, existing in such ignorance by living only for desires, creates conflicts about how to live in totality or completeness. This becomes the cause of imbalances in our psychic energy, leading to various mental ailments.

The higher the degree of dual life, the more we become enmeshed in seeking comforts for the body and mind – the more discomfort becomes a part of life, disturbing the rhythm of oneness with life. The closer we bring opposites or dualities together, the more we remain in balance or neutrality; happiness and sadness start converging as one in acceptance.

Therefore, to maintain the rhythm of life, it is important that we do not swing too much towards any extreme, but evolve into that completeness we are ultimately designed for. The key to this oneness, as I will later elaborate in detail, lies in the depth of our awareness. By increasing our awareness, consciousness awakens to the reality that we are all a part of the same intelligence-energy, gross in body, subtle in mind, core in soul, but in one single continuum.

Our main purpose is to know the meaning of existence in life through our body, mind and consciousness. We are advised that one must always maintain this beautiful machine, our body, in such a manner that self-awareness towards this obligation should remain high, in discipline, observation and alertness. Using the same process, we should keep a strong check on our thoughts and emotions, in righteousness or consonance with our value systems. This way, you transform your mind into an impartial witness and increase your awareness of your mental obligations.

Take utmost care of the body and mind in which your soul or consciousness resides, by reducing negativity. This will help in cleansing your mind and in indulging less in emotional thoughts. Your mind expands, becomes more alert and accurate. You get creatively inspired, without biased actions, with no regret or resentment and improve with good intent.

The answer to your overall well-being lies in expanding your heart to embrace the world. Love is not for one but for all. You must transcend your incessant desires, expand your heart and try to become selfless; serve as much as possible, because the ultimate answer to life lies in compassion for all.

We all have questions about the meaning of existence, life and God, and the answers are so varied, that we all become confused. The answer as given by spiritualism is that the search for the meaning of God and life are one and the same. Both God and life are hidden within you; all you need to do is realize this in absoluteness. Always look at the larger picture with an open mind.

It is postulated that realizing God and living in pure consciousness is bliss. Meaning, we can experience the existence of consciousness in the stillness, which lies beyond the chattering of the mind. It requires us to practice selfless living, unconditional love and devotion to a unified existence in oneness.

In order to realistically comprehend the liveable meaning of life as an average mortal, one has to experience and realize both worldly and spiritual existence in proper balance and moderation. Both should be in consonance with the other to stabilize the extremes of each. One is not supposed to be fully in a Buddha state of mind nor submerged in the illusions of worldly life.

Science evolves in reductionism.
The Universe evolves in expansionism.
Existence evolves in randomness.
Life evolves in awareness of that presence.

Chapter 8
The Fourth Dimension
Part I

The fourth dimension is an invisible plane of existence, a reality that lies between the physical and the spiritual realms of life. In spiritualism, the third dimension is related to the physical reality of mass, weight and volume. In this reality, we are led through life solely by the data synthesized in our minds through sensory perceptions, encompassing worldly and materialistic thoughts.

The fourth dimension is supposed to take us beyond the physical level, to the astral plane. It is a shift from physical reality to spiritual reality. External perceptions are gradually replaced by inner perceptions: awareness, creativity, intuition and imagination. It involves tuning the mind to a higher frequency where knowing increases with experiencing and the role of the thinking mind decreases.

Spiritualism postulates that in the physical dimension reality keeps changing, forming illusions in your mind and making you realize that you are limited mainly to the external world through your sensory perceptions. In this state, the mind is basically geared towards satisfying your desires and attachments, as it exists in a state of ego-consciousness. Existence here means living in dualities and so in order to absorb or express any data through the sensory organs, the mind needs to relate any characteristic to its opposite, e.g. in order to describe heat, it has to be related to cold.

When you reach a crossroads, where you feel that in spite of having wealth, comforts and family, there is still something missing; there is something serious and significant, which the mind cannot answer; it is time for you to shift into the fourth dimension to seek the higher meaning and purpose of life. The shift to the fourth dimension occurs when your mind moves from body-consciousness into spiritual consciousness. The mind then becomes habituated to living in a meditative realm, beyond thoughts of external perception. Your eyes start to look inwards instead of always looking around.

Now the mind captures creativity, intuition and imagination, which is difficult to do so otherwise. It is a reality that when we cast aside our beliefs of external perception to attain knowledge of our real self and experience self-awareness, we realize the interconnectedness of the oneness to which we all belong – the ultimate spirit.

On a spiritual level, this dimension will take you beyond the mind and consciousness into the sphere of the cosmic spirit that rules us. When functioning intellectually and indulging in a three-dimensional world, it is difficult for man and science, through thoughts and 'self-consciousness' to conceive of another dimension, which lies 'beyond' the limitations of the mind and its thoughts.

When we say, 'beyond thoughts' it means that we need to experience this higher reality through the other faculties of the mind rather than its thought processes. The essence of the fourth dimension is that it cannot be attained by the sensuous mind; it needs to be understood, practised, lived, experienced and then realized.

When you start on a journey in spiritualism, you are told that there is body, mind and spirit. This tells you that there is a possibility of another dimension, which exists beyond the intellect (which is mainly based on your past knowledge and events), which may allow you to draw fresh intelligence from the existential moment. I will try to explain this concept as logically as possible, so you can understand the depth of the concept and experience how this spirit can change your life in a wholesome manner.

Physicists, who are not able to provide any evidence for this, may say it is mystical but you need to decide yourself which answers define the distinctions between science, spiritualism and religion.

When you question yourself by asking, "Who am I?" you may answer from your mind and thoughts that you are body through flesh, and mind through thoughts, with a distinct identity. For this is what the mind lives for, and this is how we observe everything and get a sense of reality. This is how, the great French philosopher, Rene Descartes, concluded, "I think, therefore, I am." On the other hand, we are all aware that this conceptual thought of 'I am' changes constantly — physically, intellectually and psychologically with the passage of time and circumstances. Moreover, you also refer to yourself as someone or something else, sometimes, when you say 'my' body and 'my' mind, it is as if you are alluding to one of your possessions.

From childhood to who you are today, as time passes, your body and mind continue to change.

So, if it keeps changing, how can this be your real self? Reality should be changeless. Not just that, you also observe all these changes happening to your body from somewhere within, and at the same time you are also aware of how, when and what your own mind is doing. Meaning, I can witness and navigate my mind and the various movements of the body. This makes me realize that I have to be more than just mind and body, that there is something beyond.

Are you the thoughts you think? Even though everything related to you can be explained through your thoughts in words, they in turn are revealed and directed by you by being awake. Meaning, for you to think, you need to be responsive and conscious of what you are thinking; just as you cannot think while you are in deep sleep.

If I am not 'mind in thoughts', am I consciousness? What exists is a series of experiences, which takes place for every thought and act that the mind undertakes, beyond the purview of sensory perception. Meaning, behind any act, the mind collects data from the senses, knowledge from memory and bequeaths the awareness to be *conscious*, to the intellect, in that period. Therefore, your consciousness is an experience of what you have sensed, revealing the situation at hand. Wouldn't you agree that something or somebody has to be present to experience this consciousness for you to be aware of the why's and how's of what is happening?

The experiences of waking, sleeping or dreaming will come and go. As you awaken from the dissolved state of past awareness while asleep, in the same way, you need to be aware in order to become conscious of experiencing your thoughts. Every experience in the now becomes the past, what remains is the awareness within you, which does not disappear. Meaning, before and after being conscious, there has to be a 'you ' to be 'aware'.

Consciousness and thoughts come and go, with awareness remaining as that 'rememberer'. First, you need to be aware to become conscious. Therefore, you are that 'awareness' prior to everything else. Your body and mind are simply temporary tags attached to the real 'you', existing in physical form as an object. This awareness is the subject, who is observing the experience of any situation. Therefore, you remain aware before and after the experience of consciousness.

Awareness is that intelligence energy, which continuously manifests in the mind to reveal its absolute non-dual nature. It is all pervasive only differing in its degree of presence from one creature to another. Therefore, 'I am what I think' has no meaning, because before I can think, I need to be conscious and prior to that, I need to be aware. We are all one awareness of intelligence-energy existing in different degrees in each individual comprising of gross body and mind; identified by a name, as given by perceptual thoughts.

In this manner, we may say that, awareness becomes the context of the subject in the mind, and the consciousness developed therein is the content; forming your memory in the subconscious. Therefore, 'you' become the holder or the 'rememberer' of this memory in the form of your 'self-consciousness' attaching itself to the body, with a distinct identity. I repeat, the absolute, fresh intelligence-energy, which started this whole process by manifesting in your mind as awareness, becomes the subject of the presence of 'who you are'. As already explained, you cannot be an object, which changes all the time, neither can you be your defined consciousness, because it can function only after becoming aware, and later merge with your intellect to form your individuality.

To conclude, awareness is the subject of 'who you are', before as anything else – pure, absolute non-dual awareness. Therefore, in the third dimension, which is your basic physical level, you are what you think. In the fourth, you go beyond thoughts to experience and realize a higher realm, harnessing your core energy, which is: "I am that awareness; therefore, I think." This awareness is the *spirit* on which the whole of spiritualism is based.

You are that spirit in the fourth dimension, the eternal awareness that arises before anything the mind can conceive of. Your body and mind are temporary tags attached to you, as they last only one cycle of birth and death. In reality, both awareness and consciousness are distinct from each other. Consciousness emerges only because of the prior luminous intelligence-energy manifesting in the mind as awareness. This awareness remains absolute in its own identity and in no way is dependent upon or affected by consciousness.

Our basic ultimate constituent is this intelligence-energy called awareness, which our consciousness is dependent upon. After that, on receiving data from thoughts generated by sensory perception and intuitive intelligence from awareness, the mind, experiences and transmits the same through the intellect by means of thoughts, words, language and actions of the body and mind. The responsibility for all this is placed upon our individuality or what is referred to as self-consciousness.

Awareness in the fourth dimension is that spiritual energy, claimed to be, 'who' you really are. It is that intelligence energy continuously manifesting in your mind and in all others, revealing its absolute non-dual nature of being the same in everything and everyone. It may differ in degree, but it remains the same in quality. It is only during the final stages of self-realization, when mind and body dissolve into pure consciousness, it becomes total awareness. If you subtract all the layers of dualities from your consciousness, what remains is a sense of total awareness of pure consciousness. This determines the presence of who you are.

Pure cosmic energy is thoughtless, non-dual, absolute and potential energy. It manifests in the mind as inert intelligence-energy in the form of the Witnessing Self to make your mind conscious of every act and thought. In the mind, this energy separates to exist in and experience dualities in opposites. In order for the mind to function, it is essential for it to relate to opposites to come to any conclusion.

Therefore, the mind, receiving its perceptions from the sensory organs can function only in duality and that too only in your self-interest.

In discerning and discriminating between any two dual characteristics, it chooses what it wants or desires. In this manner, a false sense of self emerges, which is called 'ego'. This ego thrives upon self-esteem and is constantly in wanting mode of more and more. It is also responsible for creating conflicts, which thrive on anxiety, despair and mental agony.

As long as the mind stays limited to the third dimension, the 'ego' will persist, designed to make you flourish in the materialistic world. Therefore, on one end, you have the false self, emerging from your greedy mind in the form of ego and on another, you have the real Self, as the spiritual mind emerging from awareness in the form of consciousness. In order to exist in the world, both are required to fulfil their purpose and journey.

Consciousness from the subtle mind becomes the pure Witnessing Self, watching all that is going on in the mind through awareness, making you aware of positive and negative, right and wrong, to balance the ego. However, on attaching it to the body and mind, is enmeshed in layers of dualities, which reduce it to the aspects of personality in self-consciousness. It is your common sense, personal power, individuality or your 'self-consciousness' which determines what to let go of or accept in the material world until it leaps back to its original state of pure consciousness.

Your individuality arises from your consciousness, which is why it has been given so much importance. The separation of this aware energy into the dualities of the mind is what makes you anxious, weak and dependent in 'self-consciousness'. This continues until you reach purity in self-realization, and can exist in parity with total awareness with the absolute and non-dual.

The consciousness, which emerges from awareness, reveals that there is no such thing as an individual. It is only the presence of this spirit or energy in the singular, which is where everything like matter and intelligence emerges from and dissolves back. This is what the law of conservation of energy states: telling us that we are pure energy, neither created nor destroyed. It only changes in shapes, sizes and forms, where nothing extra be added or subtracted.

This completeness and oneness of energy is referred to as *Brahman* — the ultimate reality of which we are all a part, existing as timeless, changeless, spaceless, and limitless energy in total awareness. The individual mind is a part of this cosmic awareness, and each mind is connected through its thoughts with every other mind. Everyone's mind is in constant communication through this cosmic link with every other mind, whatever be the location of another, in whichever part of the world. This grid of consciousness is what is referred to as the unified field of consciousness.

The mind is that supreme organ which permits intuitive connection by awareness to link the past, present and the future in our thoughts. At the same time, the mind also regulates the organs of the body, voluntarily or otherwise through internal and external perception, for us to be in accord with our external surroundings in order for our system to function smoothly. It is only your mind in desire, functioning in self-interest mode, which disturbs this synchronization, which needs to be, stabilized.

You should note that the mind perceives everything mainly through sense perceptions of objects. While you are reading, however, you as the subject are aware that the mind is the medium, which is reading. You also know that this presence of awareness is who you are. All else is impermanent or apparent, it just comes and goes. This is the reason why knowing the Self is the most important thing in spiritualism, especially when you wish to venture into the fourth dimension – from the physical self to the spiritual one.

To repeat, this pure potential energy on manifesting in the mind becomes the awareness of who you are; the non-dual absolute being the source from which consciousness emerges in your body and mind. Consciousness appears merely as a blip in the realm of the absolute, relating itself to objects, becoming your identity, uniqueness or personality, until it is able to self-realize in pure consciousness.

Our sense of individuality arises through such series of experiences with objects.

The mind is all that we have; we are supposed to use the mind and not be used by it. However, in physical reality, the reverse takes place, you become a victim of your own mind, attached to external desires, which leads to a vicious cycle of pleasure and pain. You live within the illusions of your superficial perceptions. It is like watching a movie and getting so mesmerized by the drama that you start thinking it is real, forgetting you are only watching what is on a screen.

Mind: You are what you think.
Spirit: I am when I do not think.
Mind: Life is in duality.
Spirit: Life is in oneness.
Mind: I am the doer.
Spirit: The doer, doing and done are all the same.
Mind: God is our lord and almighty.
Spirit: You and God are one.

Part II

The philosophical or ontological point of view of the fourth dimension, explains that the mind faces certain limitations in whatever direction it may take. However, it further elaborates, that in order to revive the state from where it originated, the same mind, when it evolves and shifts from the physical into the realm of the spirit.

Since sensory perception is very physical in character, it becomes imperative to first accrue knowledge of the Self, know 'who I am' before proceeding any further in the area of spirituality. The limitations of the third dimension are primarily because external perception restricts the mind only to the past or into the future, focused only on objects. The present or the now can never be captured by the perceptive mind. However, the spiritual awareness of the moment, which is the mother of all thoughts, exists only in the present. It is this very awareness in the spontaneity of the now that is responsible for creativity, intuition and imagination, which enters the mind in a flash. In order to reach the fourth dimension, one must recognize the fact that awareness is the source and presence of everything. It is the basis of all other data released by the mind.

What you need to know is that 'you' come prior to everything else that takes place in the psychic computer called your mind. Consciousness is a state of being awake in awareness and it is only you who can experience this fact. The state of awakening may go to sleep but awareness continues unabated. Consciousness emerges from non-dual pure awareness, but when it identifies with objects, it becomes dual in mind as 'self-consciousness' giving rise to individuality. Behind these layers of dualities enfolded around your real self, lies the core of your being present as pure consciousness in conformity with the non-dual state of absolute awareness. Awareness or the fourth dimension is related to the now or the presence of the mind, linking the cosmic source to the Self.

To summarize, awareness makes the mind aware, it impels it to become conscious in order to experience physical reality, the sum total of which forms our consciousness. Consciousness, in turn becomes responsible for determining the net result of all the neural functions of the mind in forming separate images for every situation. In its absolute aspect, it remains as the Witnessing Self, becoming the subject of who we are, in total awareness. In its relative aspect, it attaches itself to the object of body and mind to determine and experience that entire mind in ego-consciousness, forming your individuality. This continues through umpteen cycles of birth and death, until the body and mind decompose to become one with the absolute Witnessing Self in Self-Realization.

Allow me to go through the above assertions again, in a different manner. Let us start with; When you say or think this is my mind and body, it means you are something more than that. Because your 'my and mine' can only be an attachment to a possession of yours. When you explore your mind, asking, 'who am I' your intellect throws up only the past in the form of thoughts from past knowledge. Further, you also notice that you can be aware of your own mind and thoughts and monitor the manner in which it behaves and functions. Therefore, your real self has to be different than all that you keep observing.

What is it that makes you self-aware for your mind to be conscious of how it thinks and acts? Consciousness forms your individuality or uniqueness by witnessing your mind and thoughts. However, are you that? No! Because in order for consciousness to function, there is something prior to that, for you to be aware, become conscious and then think. It means 'what' you are is your consciousness and the component of this source from where consciousness emerges, is 'who' you are while the body and mind reflects 'how' you are.

This pure absolute energy is the ultimate component present in you; it is a part of that Creator. It is the manifested radiance of potential, absolute energy, illuminating your mind, turning into the kinetic energy called awareness. Therefore, Creator and Creation are the same, except that the former is complete in totality whereas the latter being a part of the whole infinity, in the same quality, needs to revive back into totality from its stint in dual living.

You are indeed of the same in quality and are a part of that infinite source of eternal Awareness, residing in the mind, covered in layers of consciousness, separated into dualities of good/bad, positive/negative, God/Devil, etc. The fourth dimension is the shift of the core of your being from the physical to the spiritual. You may then continue into the level of the fifth dimension where you literally dissolve in pure consciousness or total awareness.

This is the Buddha state of mind, but this sort of absolute existence is very rare and is a visionary state. It occurs when you dissolve your mind and body in consciousness, spirit or soul in purity. It is to be in total awareness while merging with that non-dual energy. Spiritual enlightenment, in those ancient days, was claimed to be realized by Buddha, Jesus and a few others. It is possible to achieve this state only through selfless living, with unconditional love and forgiveness, where there is no separation between 'mine' and 'yours'.

From this conclusion, we arrive at the doctrine that declares, 'I am That' or 'Thou art That'. The common misunderstanding here is that we start presuming we are God, due to the presence of the awareness within us, especially when we read and hear that the Creator is the Creation. Yes, we as objects, existing in body, mind and intellect are a part of the same subject, equal in quality, but we remain only as a part of that completeness, because our energies are separated into dualities, until we reach the fifth dimension.

Our mind is divided into two sections – on one end we have the absolute, non-dual energy as Awareness or the Witnessing Self, and on the other, we have perceptual, dual energy in what we call 'ego', separating everything that our sensory organs perceive and conceive of, into dualities, as 'self-consciousness'. We need to unite the two separated ends of dualities, bring them back to their original self; until then, we remain only as a part and not as the whole.

Awareness, the fourth dimension, is the presence of our pure being. It can be experienced only in the now, whereas the mind persists in thinking thoughts of the past or the future. This is why, in order to realize the presence of our being, it becomes necessary to obtain self-knowledge in order to be self-aware, live meditatively from one moment to the next and self-realize in experiential and existential living – the oneness of who we really are.

From the above, you may notice, science is not equipped to conjecture on the subject of Awareness, as it is neither physical nor can it be measured. Science deals mainly with the physicality of any object in its methodology of reductionism whereas the fourth dimension is really an extension of the third, leading us towards the fifth dimension. It is only then that we fully realize our mind, body and soul as explained above in eternal enlightenment in pure consciousness. Since all this resists being proven, the study of the spirit remains mysterious. If it is separatism that signifies the third dimension, it is awareness in the present that moves the mind, body and soul towards the fourth dimension. Each dimension reflects how we evolve in the mental realm, becoming the force behind our reaching one stage and then another.

Awareness is about intuition, imagination and creativity; from mechanical thought processes to becoming aware. It is best achieved in a meditative state as explained in detail later on. We need to realize that God is not a separate entity in the manner propounded by every religion. God is a part of everything that exists and a part of you, the only difference being, in us, this supreme energy is separated into extremes, with the other end being the Devil.

God is present in all of us as total awareness, not as a person but in the form of Supreme Reality representing love and light in the form of energy. Therefore, the fourth dimension is a shift from one to the other, in continuum of who and what we are. God is not outside but within us, where no evidence is required, but only realization of that awakening of the real Self.

All enlightened souls, though they were not religious, taught us about this mental realm of awareness in some way or the other, communicating through their love and selfless actions. As time passed, their teachings were changed from what they were initially, becoming corrupted by traditions, beliefs and dogmas. In this manner, less enlightened people made use of this knowledge, converting it into what we call religion today.

One factor, we need to bear in mind is that we do not need to make any abrupt changes in moving from one dimension to another. It is a gradual process, totally dependent on the individual soul. It depends on how he is directed by his thoughts and awareness to gradually evolve and shift from the lower to the higher dimension. This is the essence and realization of such a shift in our consciousness.

When we reside in the third dimension, we simply react to a situation and continue to think about the same later. Our reactions and responses to a stimulus are governed by past thoughts and memories. When we introspect deeply, we realize what is happening to our 'self-consciousness' is mainly connected to our experiences of what we perceive. We experience everything that is perceived internally and externally, before the mind makes any inference. Science is able to explain only the physical or mechanical perception aspect of our external world and not what the mind experiences.

Spirituality says that until an awakening takes place and you understand the context or the subject of who you are, you remain ignorant.

You require this spiritual awakening, this shift into the next dimension to experience and realize, as explained in various ways, in all three of my books. Moreover, you need to further understand the state of total awareness, which blossoms in the fifth dimension. Until then we are limited to being a bundle of psychic experiences in this mortal existence, chained to 'self-consciousness', while living in spiritual ignorance.

Life, is a series of experiences while we exist, where the concept of memory states that the experiencer and the one witnessing within, has to be the same. How else can memory be present or be interpreted? Death, on the other hand is defined, when the experiencer existing in the body and mind ceases to experience any further.

The persistent demands of desire and attachments overwhelm existence in the third dimension.

Ignorance occurs when our 'self-consciousness' is influenced and pressurized by the mind to attachments and desires leading to cycles of pleasure and pain. The mind therefore, is controlled on one side by your external perceptions leading towards desires and on the other, by your inner perception – that is consciousness, illumined by awareness.

The same consciousness undergoes various cycles of birth and death until it reaches that stage of pure consciousness equal or in parity to that of total awareness.

When the mind is wandering, quieten it.
When the mind is chattering; still it.
When the mind is unconscious; awaken it.

Part III

Spiritualism deals with the perceptual, non-perceptual and transcendental knowledge of the mind. Not only that, it gives us insight into the nature of Ultimate Reality. Self-knowledge to self-realization, spiritualism is concerned with meditative living in the transcendental stage, rather than in its study.

In spiritualism, the guru or master, is only supposed to guide the way and show the right direction. The rest is dependent on an individual's intellect and his consciousness to sculpt the way and pattern of life he wishes for himself. The essence of spiritual knowledge is embedded in our self-luminous consciousness.

This luminosity cannot be transferred by anybody. On the physical level, it is unaware of its own self, and this is where a guru is needed but only to indicate the direction. Awareness can be manifested, experienced and realized only by the individual himself. He is the one who needs to seek that space and freedom to narrow the gap of dualities, which his mind creates.

The mind as an object can think and perceive on its own, but it is the Aware Self, which illuminates the mind through experience. This radiance in itself is the subject of who we are and not the object that we possess as body and mind. No guru or master can manage these states for another. The reason being: the Self, God and Guru are all within. When the self attains self-knowledge in knowing that we are all but one continuum of energy, the external guru vanishes and dissolves within him as one in realization of the awareness of Ultimate Reality.

When anyone evolves from the physical realm into the fourth dimension, he is required to first and foremost understand the reality behind the mind, body and spirit. Firstly, one is required to gain self-knowledge about the spirit and then go further into understanding self-awareness and self-realization. Let us investigate what exactly self-knowledge is, why it is essential and how it should be exercised.

As we know, the mind is the supreme structure in the human body. It narrates our experiences in the form of thoughts for everything that can be perceived internally or externally. However, being or our presence in body and mind cannot simply be a thought. You cannot simply understand and comprehend 'who you are' from mere thoughts. You need the right knowledge and understanding to know your identity as an aware being. It is only then that you will be able to align your sense of self to the consciousness of what you are. It is awakening from ignorance that leads you to your liberation from thoughts into the fourth dimension.

Self-knowledge should be studied when you are curious about whether we are body, mind and intellect or something more. The process normally starts when you realize that your mind is being watched and guided by a witness. The urge to perceive this witness apart from your thoughts arises with the knowledge that the mind needs to be aware to become conscious; that we are more than just body and mind.

No one yet has been able to answer where self-awareness originates from and whether it settles into memory, as past awareness or thoughts in the subconscious mind in the form of consciousness. Scientists first presumed that this self-awareness came from the cortex region of the mind but were soon proved wrong. Spiritualists claim that awareness is non-dual, absolute, pure and pristine cosmic energy, which manifests in the mind when you are alert and observant in the present moment. The mind as a receiver of this intelligence energy becomes conscious and then separates this energy into dualities or opposites in self-interest by discerning and choosing to fulfil its wants and desires. Self-knowledge involves the study of understanding this spirit, going beyond the physical thoughts of the third dimension, deeper into consciousness and awareness in order to reach the fourth level.

Once you realize that thoughts are limited merely to sensory perceptions, the phenomenon of your constantly swaying from one dual characteristic to another — from pleasure to pain or into conflicts of anger, anxiety, fear and despair — will decrease. You will definitely wish to learn more about self-knowledge, for all that it can teach you – how to go beyond physical problems and awaken into a higher realm.

The problem faced today is that most of us who seek to know this reality of who 'I' am are being carried away by the supernatural connotations of 'I am that' or I am the same as God. They start blindly learning the final stages of the supreme reality or presume that they are self-realized, trying to seek enlightenment, from one ashram to another. There is nothing to seek, for seeking is just a desire. The fact of the matter is that yes, spiritually, we all contain the same absolute non-dual energy, present in all of us in one continuum, where we are all connected as one. The difference is that this core absolute energy is covered in layers of self-interest separating this absoluteness into the dualities of God/Devil, positive/negative, truth/lies, etc. We need to understand that it is intense spiritual living with awareness, experience and realization, which expands your consciousness towards that oneness of who and what you really are.

We linger as a part of this absolute, equal in quality, because energy can neither be created nor destroyed but only change in character. This energy needs to revert to its original state of absoluteness. For this, you undergo numerous cycles of birth and death, until you liberate yourself from the burden of dualities and self-realize your spirit in pure consciousness. In this manner, the Ultimate Reality of who we are lies in accruing experiential knowledge of the supra sensible and to understand the supreme aspect of our being or presence. Therefore, to realize the final stage of this journey in self-realization or pure consciousness is not as easy as it is sometimes presumed to be. It is extremely rare and only a few have achieved this state of total awareness.

In the process of attaining spiritual knowledge, we encounter the following constructs: the knower (self), the process of knowing (mind) and the known (the object). What we need to understand here is that it is only through the Self that you may know anything; it is only in the Self that you find the culmination and solutions for all doubt, delusion and deception.

What is happening commonly though is we try to understand deep spiritual concepts through someone else's knowledge and experience, gossip or books. Since most of us do not practise what we have learnt by imbibing this knowledge into our lives, we are not experienced enough to realize and soon forget what we have learnt.

This way, many of us, in spite of knowing about self-knowledge from others, remain in the body consciousness of our ego in the third dimension.

For the fourth dimension, spiritual practices with personal effort or *Sadhana* is essential. No knowledge is complete unless experienced by the Self. Therefore, *tantra* and yoga are required to assist you in this existential or experiential journey in realizing self-knowledge, so you may enjoy the worlds of both materialism and spiritualism. You need to accept both dualities with grace; indulge, outgrow and transform in awareness to reach that focal point of health, wealth, peace, and comfort in body, mind, and soul.

Self-awareness, as explained in this book is necessary, because unless the mind is disciplined you will not be able to empower yourself to overcome the lust and greed of sensuous perceptions. You will realize life; not only objectively but also experience the subjective essence of awareness by taking each action in life sensitively and whole-heartedly.

Such discipline of the mind will bring you to awareness; make you proficient in using the mind and not be used by it. Usually, we are the victims of our minds because of attachments and desires, with the mind churning out one desire after another. To counter this, the meditative power of inner perception through awareness is able to counteract the sensuous power of external perception. Meditation as spiritual *sadhana*, plays a very important role in this process.

I have always felt that life is a cosmic joke played upon us. It is like a seesaw, swinging from this to that and back; say from pleasure to pain. For that matter, if the Devil were not there, where was the need for God? If no one lied, would the truth have taken birth? Those who have realized the tricks of our Universe are the mavericks. They have learnt how to acknowledge both dualities with respect, centring them back into one.

The energy that flows out of this centring philosophy does not make you a Hindu or a Muslim but someone who understands love and forgiveness as one. When you witness your thoughts, you are aware. When you think from your mind, you reason. When you combine them both, you become ONE, not to judge but to accept.

When the mind starts seeking, it expresses desire but when the mind is watchful, observant and alert, it becomes aware in the search for truth. You cannot desire the truth, you can find it, and you can feel it and you can experience it. For truth happens in the now but the mind cannot be in the now, it can only exist in the past and the future.

When you are limited to the third dimension, you are off-centred. Your life is a seesaw, swinging from one dual factor to another, from positive to negative, truth to untruth, pleasure to pain, etc. You continue existing on such a plane in which you do not realize the stage of reality you are in or the ignorance of your own mind, surrounded as you are by desires, attachments, choices and conflicts. Even your natural sleep gets disturbed. Your mind is hyperactive; you require tranquilizers not only to sleep but also to calm your mind.

Then emerges the philosophy of centring, not to go to heaven or hell, but to accept all dual factors with grace; observe in alertness to be aware and indulge to outgrow and go beyond to transform. Transformation is to go beyond 'self-consciousness', into the realm of pure awareness where you realize that the truth lies not in making choices between good or bad in your self-interest but in accepting both good and bad with respect. It is only in awareness, that there is no struggle, surrender, control or suppression. Awareness enables you to transcend what you do not approve of, effortlessly. This is what I mean by the transformation of any soul from the third dimension to the fourth. This book is dedicated to awareness, with utmost respect. The core essence of my being is blessed in leading you towards that journey into the fourth dimension.

The fifth dimension is a vision, that too for the very select few. It is for those who wish to realize enlightenment, where there is zero conflict in their consciousness. They need to be ready to dissolve their mind and body to selfless living in unconditional love and forgiveness. There is no desire, no wanting or clinging to somebody. Such souls never think of the past or future. They realize the present, in the presence of the now. In awareness of the supreme reality, there is nothing to seek. One exists, but never thinks of tomorrow, since one is in total awareness.

You are in-between, on one side, you have your perceptual thoughts demanding their desires and on another end you have the Buddha or Christ.

You require centring. Bring your separated energies closer and see how miracles happen in your life.

Choiceless consciousness is total awareness.

Chapter 9
Choiceless Awareness

Choice is a prerogative of the mind. In order to decide between this and that in duality, the mind makes a choice, thinking that is the best option to guard one's self-interest. For the materialistic world, the mind is everything and choices are necessary; spirituality seeks a no-mind zone where the mind and choices are considered as the cause of all conflicts.

Whenever there is a preference, there will be a choice; you will not be able to interpret any situation subjectively. Even before understanding a situation, your mind would have already made its choice and that too drawing from past knowledge. For one who lives with desires, choice is imperative. A person who understands and knows, limits his choices. He allows his awareness to flow in creativity, intuition and inspiration in choicelessness.

He understands that the mind can function only in ego and duality in order to judge and choose and in return, it becomes conditioned by such factors. If we ignore the rantings of the mind, we will know and understand that in actuality, there is nothing right or wrong. What is right for me may be wrong for the other, making your choice only an illusion.

The basic purpose of the mind is analysis, reasoning and choosing. No great man has ever said that his greatness is due to his mind; each has reported that inspiration just came, from the totality of life in creativity and awareness. The mind merely mulls over facts to choose and discriminate. The mind only chooses happiness and gain, but also invites sadness and loss because you simply cannot separate energy for your own benefit. Both heaven and hell need to be accepted in totality. You need to surrender to choicelessness.

An animal lives by its natural instincts, without choice, not knowing how to discriminate or judge, or decide whether it is happy or sad. Besides possessing intellect, a human being is conscious of his self and his world. However, since he is not fully aware, he can never be completely correct in his decision-making. Taking a cue from rational thought, he believes in cutting, dividing and then choosing his subject. For him it then becomes 'my idea', 'my thing' and 'my life', through his individual perceptions and choices.

A spiritually aware person is a balanced person. Observant and alert, he prefers not to choose by remaining in the centre. For, if you choose one, you are bound to experience the other. Say, if you choose happiness, sadness is bound to follow. One is inherent in the other. Both happiness and sadness are a state of mind. If life provides one extreme, the other is intrinsically built into it.

Happiness is your nature; you cannot seek or desire it. Go with the flow in awareness and oneness; prefer the centre of each dual force. Do not choose;

try to traverse the middle path, because choice means pitting one thing against the other. Try to be neutral, upright and centred. Instead of choosing, be a witness while taking an action, so you may prove to be stronger than your happiness or sadness, and eventually grow out of them. It is in witnessing that you will invite awareness into your being; it will make you understand the totality of any situation.

Further, when you make a choice, your mind has to think, which makes you react from a fixed or past point of view, opening the door to conflict. Choosing between this and that is always an unpredictable proposition, depending on moods, whims and fancies, leading to further conflicts. Imagine the role choice plays – choosing, wanting and then battling in conflict, especially when the results are not to your satisfaction. However, as suggested earlier, if one practises discipline in action, one avoids the conflicts that arise out of making a choice. To do so, if one has to respond to any stimulus, one needs to learn the art of being alert, observant, watchful, sensitive and spontaneous. Then, one's response or actions would be proactive and creative, rather than being reactive.

In one of his books, Osho has mentioned Socrates, one of the founders of Western philosophy: "Someone asked Socrates where he would like to go, and Socrates said, 'I don't know whether there are hell and heaven. I don't know whether they are there or not, but I will not choose between them. My only prayer will be this; allow me to be alert wherever I am. Let me be fully aware wherever I am. Whether it is hell or heaven is irrelevant."

In materialistic existence, choice plays an important role; the mind is demanding, always selecting between 'this or that' only in self-interest. In spiritual or empirical living, the less we choose the better. We are required to be balanced and centred, where our spontaneity in the now, rather than our thoughts, determine the action that needs to be taken.

Choices are never constant; they keep changing within space and time. Any choice also has the tendency to cause damage, because under any circumstances, we normally choose an option in reaction to a given situation, using the logic that comes out of biased thoughts. Since, our choices are related only to thoughts of self-interest there are chances of confusion and conflicts.

As explained earlier, an animal lives naturally within his environment, using his instincts, without any conflict; but a human being possesses a consciousness to discern, discriminate and choose, which makes him different. However, if he acts in the awareness of the now, he becomes proactive and creative rather than reacting through biased thoughts.

Therefore, be proactive by using either natural inbuilt awareness or by constantly practicing observation, alertness, discipline and spontaneous action in any situation. Do not allow your biased thoughts to interfere. Welcome new intuitive intelligence into your mind for your knowledge to expand, rather than depending on past thoughts. This way, you will not react to any situation, but act in awareness of only that particular moment. Accept everything in totality; indulge to outgrow and transform any situation, without feeling any compulsion or pressure.

It is said that there are two primary physical emotions – love and fear; both are activated in our minds as a reaction to a situation. That is, if there is no cause for a reaction, there is no love or fear. Both connect to the past and the emotion created, becomes a reaction. Physical emotions as such, are nothing but agitated or excited bundles of thoughts, put into motion. Love as a physical reaction is very common — say, because of attraction to someone, one reacts in love. Similarly, fear usually emerges as a distressed emotion and is aroused during times of danger.

Further, lust and possessiveness are often mistaken for love, e.g. the desire of a man for a woman arising out of sexuality or a feeling of ownership over that person, are nothing but physical reactions. Love, in this case is relative, either in the degree of lust or possessiveness; it has the tendency to morph into its opposite at any given moment. When faced with limitations, expectations or duality, physical love can change any moment to its opposite, say hatred, if ideal conditions are not fulfilled. This love mainly arises in self-interest; it is more like a demand, possessiveness or a calculation of returns. Love, which is free, unbound and not directed by the mind to choose or react, which just flows in action, in leaps and bounds – this unconditional love, is called absolute love.

While emotionally dependent, we remain in ego-consciousness, making choices that are self-centred, and so we react to any situation in a biased manner, which invariably leads to conflicts. This is because thought-impulses coming out of the auto mode of the subconscious into the conscious mind are clouded by past knowledge and charged with emotions. Therefore, how we interact with any situation is of prime importance to avoid negativity.

We need to have control over our actions, and with astute alertness and clarity, allow awareness to flow into us as creative intuition, merging with the intellect to manifest as proper action. This will gradually make us realize that our response to any situation enacted in this manner, is far superior to merely reacting to what our thoughts may have directed us to do.

It is space and just space in this space-less, timeless, limitless Universe.

Only when you perceive space do you realize that you are here and there in dualities.

Chapter 10
Dual and Non-dual

Life cannot exist in a single state; each state has to have its opposite, in much the same way as the fact that you cannot live alone, you have to have someone or something to relate to. Opposites are necessary; meaning, for existence, duality is required. You will notice life has a certain pattern – good/bad, male/female, God/Devil, day/night, etc. We all live according to this pattern and the moment we try to separate one from another the rhythm of existence is disturbed.

We are often told, "This is bad, this is right and that is wrong, don't do this," etc. It is not for us to judge what is right or wrong. As one needs to be serious, one also needs to laugh, so for the sake of totality and oneness in life, opposites are necessary for us to understand the meaning of life. As you travel along the path of duality, you discover that opposites are two ends of their intrinsic oneness. One is inherent in the other, and both together form the whole. It is awareness that helps us cross from one to another or to draw them towards the centre, back into oneness.

One cannot exist without the other, like day and night. Truth would not have existed, if we did not know how to lie, there would be no need for an external God, without the presence of the Devil. Until you experience both, you cannot become aware of this phenomenon. In fact, there would be no need for awareness to manifest in the mind. The need for awareness arises to bring in rhythm and cohesion between the two. Of course, religion would never agree, as it is bound by belief, never to accept evil or Satan.

Moreover, whatever any spiritual guru might say, if you do not have ego or desire, your very own 'I' would disappear and the term 'ego-less' would lose its meaning. Both are simply different sides of the same coin. It is only when these two join as one that we find absolute reality. The absolute energy never splits, it simply separates; the further they are from each other, more you will be in worldly illusions. The closer you are towards their origin, the centre, your spirit will be in cohesion, balanced and in harmony and this can be made possible only through spiritual awareness.

Spirituality revolves around awareness and oneness. All that exists is one. *Brahman*, has also been confirmed by science through Quantum Mechanics as energy. It can change into different forms from matter to energy and back, but the sum total remains constant and in continuum. This energy cannot be divided it can only separate into different forms.

Absolute energy manifests in the mind as two aspects, absolute in awareness and separated as relative/opposites or dual. In reality they are one and in continuum, but only separated at opposite ends. In order to exist one has to encounter and experience both, because without the presence of one the need for the other does not arise.

In this manner, without the Devil, the need for God disappears, but they both are in fact one and part of the same absolute energy. Through experience, one can realize how to bring these separated energies back to their centre through awareness. Centring or Oneness, in fact is visionary, for it can be fully realized only in Self Realization in total awareness or Pure Consciousness. Buddha, Jesus, and a few others are supposed to have realized such a state. *Moksha* (liberation) is attained when you are free of duality or opposites and this is possible only when body and mind dissolve into spirit as One.

Our job, even if we cannot realize total awareness, is to bring dualities as close as possible towards their centre. This way we shall become more balanced and aware and will be able to counter both good and bad with equal respect and not get agitated/excited/disturbed/anxious and so on. Say if you become aware of what you consider bad, you are then bound to introspect, accept in awareness and outgrow gradually to transform from acceptance in grace, rather than from conflict.

Awareness teaches us how to deal effectively with each duality, not in refusal or rejection, but in acceptance, indulgence and transformation. If we reject, how can we become aware? In addition, when we experience awareness in its entirety, opposites no longer hold any meaning. We accept all as one.

Duality arises from your unconscious mind. It is for you to awaken out of this ignorance, rouse your awareness into totality and oneness, and decide which the real 'you' is. Factors like identity or religion (for e.g. I may say I am a Hindu, but I was not born as one, I was given this religion) are things we were conditioned into, like many other ideals were ingrained into our minds since childhood. We therefore usually live through that past conditioned mind, forcing it onto the present.

We remain imprisoned in the past through our minds and force the same onto our family or progeny. We need to be aware of our pure consciousness, that subtle Witnessing Self, which tells us who we are really.

Each of us is that awareness, the spirit or energy, the

non-dual potential absolute form, existing in the form of a Witnessing Self. The creative process in the cycle of birth and death is actually meant for existential and experiential realization for any individual soul to liberate itself from the bondage of duality.

Absolute awareness, after manifesting in the mind becomes aware, as a result of which, the mind becomes conscious and separates into opposites in order to choose between the two for its survival or self-interest. Gradually 'self-consciousness' forms out of the experiences one undergoes. The reason being, existence can only exist within opposites: day/night, God/Devil, truth/untruth, etc. Both are intrinsic and inherent to the other. Such an existence continues in various cycles of birth and death, until 'self-consciousness' becomes fully aware in Total Awareness to Self-Realize in Pure Consciousness, which is known as God. Hence, the connotation of the term 'I am That'. At this stage, body, mind and soul become One; there is no duality and only oneness remains in equilibrium. It is a visionary state and realized in the lives of Buddha or Jesus, the reason for them being referred to as God.

In this manner, the absolute potential energy experiences three layers of existences:

a. Illusory or dual
b. Empirical or experiential
c. Absolute existence

However, they all are the same; each one has the Absolute as the content in accordance with the degree of its individual awareness, besides body-mind energy. Therefore, awareness is constructed with a foundation, which is a triad of:

a. The Object as matter, in the form of gross, mass energy.
b. Individuality in the form of dual, intangible energy in self-consciousness.
c. The Absolute as potential, non-dual energy.

Similarly, God and the Devil are not two beings, whatever religious masters may say. They both reside in us; if God has created me, then the Devil, the cause of evil is also in me, which means, God has also created the Devil. They are just two sides of the same reality, because without the Devil, we might not need God. Religion though, remains in conflict between the two, we are pulled from each end, and the ends never seem to meet.

Therefore, we remain ignorant and trapped in duality, fearing both at different times and under different circumstances. If we accept them as one, there is no more duality. In a state of freedom and awareness, indulging in both, we can decide on our own, which journey we are to take and freely drop what we do not approve of. There is no conflict, no fear, no special effort, only acceptance in love and harmony.

It does not make a difference whether you are a Muslim, Hindu or Christian. These tags are only a façade, because we are all the same. Though we have different names and various identities, we are born with the same dualities of lust to greed. You may keep searching for peace in different philosophies or religions, convert or re-convert, but internally, only your own spiritual awareness can awaken you to the reality of who you truly are.

Please remember, what I am expressing is applicable

to those of us who are somewhat in control of ourselves — mentally, physically and emotionally, — and especially to those who are not rigid in their mindset. Simply indulge, outgrow and transform: one needs to rise and transcend beyond thought. We need to be aware of what lies behind our perceptions, in not having false apprehensions or mistaking apparent reality as real or the ultimate truth.

This becomes difficult, when a person is physically, emotionally, financially or mentally shattered. In periods of agony, we see such desolation, that we seek emotional and mental support from any source, authority or leader. Here, the person gives up his freedom, finds temporary refuge or shelter and obtains relief. Such people are the chief victims of organized cults and unconsciously live in constant fear and doubt.

Duality arises when we cut and separate every thought in our mind into this and that, and try to choose. Spiritual awareness tells you not to separate anything into two, just accept everything, become choiceless, and be alert. If God and you are separate, no preacher can bring you together, he will only keep preaching to further his own interests. Only you, acting from within, experiencing through your awareness, will be able to move closer towards the idea of the world and the divine as one, because divinity itself is the world.

Negativity and you are also one and it is a part of you. If it is there, it is simply there. Do not try to force yourself out of it — you might just suppress and bury it deeper within yourself. Accept it with astute awareness, do not be blind to it, and make the situation worse. For you to gain maturity, you need to let it dissolve naturally and simply observe its harmful effects. In this way, your negativity is bound to reduce.

Preachers will tell you to discard your ego and negativity. I would say, flow with it, but be aware, become true to your own self. Gradually, you will start witnessing how your ego plays games with you, becoming a mirror of you, taking control of your mind as your master. Your mind should always be your slave and nothing else.

Awareness treats the mind as a part of the body. It controls and rules the mind. It is that invisible witness – thinking, listening and talking through the mind – accessing the mind. In the mind, awareness is the real you, acting as finite consciousness to perceive and experience the nature of form in objectivity. When formless, it reverts into total awareness, into its true absolute nature as the limitless, infinite, eternal energy in the unified field of consciousness.

There is nothing that is right or wrong, good or bad; it is all a perception that resides in your ego and in your dual mind. If you have been blessed with the power of choice and discrimination, you are also blessed with the power of dissolving these two with awareness, and removing the conflict between the two. Accept things as they occur, but in awareness; connect more deeply inwards, so your true self is able to guide you in the direction meant for you.

To sum up, the Self as intelligence-energy, is who we are. It manifests as self-consciousness in dual life, and pure consciousness in the Absolute. This absolute intelligence-energy enlightens through awareness, is intangible and supernatural, beyond logic and science, hence the name given to it is 'spirit'. Spiritualism is therefore, based on such a 'science' of consciousness.

Consciousness, also referred to as the self, is present in all of us. It is indivisible but prevails in different degrees. It is like the sky; we can focus only on a part of it through our eyes, but in totality, it remains indivisible – as infinite consciousness. Through our self or ego-consciousness, we may try to cut and divide it but in itself, it remains complete, in a continuum.

In this context, God is defined as 'the one existing in pure consciousness or total awareness in bliss'. Since it is present in a continuum in all of us, whosoever manages to reach this height is blessed by being referred to as God; like for e.g. Jesus Christ, the Buddha and Krishna.

Erwin Schrödinger, an eminent Austrian physicist and Nobel Prize winner, presented his ideas, known as Schrödinger's paradox, in *What is Life* where he wrote: "Each individual consciousness is only a manifestation of a unitary consciousness, pervading the Universe that is, in the sense, a sort of God." The feeling of divisibility or plurality is only an illusion or a paradox, which Hindus refer to as '*Maya*'.

In relative, the mind experiences dualities.
In absolute, the mind experiences the source.

Chapter 11
The Power of the Absolute

There is a distinct relationship between reality, creation, existence, truth and awareness. They all converge into one as a whole. In a similar manner, quantum physics declares all that exists in our Universe is nothing but energy in one continuum, complete in itself. Likewise, we are a part of this, as energy, absolute and complete, but are required to reinstate our separated energies to its origin, its totality as One.

Understanding this phenomenon or its applicability may differ for each individual. The philosophy of the Absolute is complex and is not easily realizable by an average person in its totality. Most of us continue to live and enjoy the fruits of duality. To understand the path of absolute reality, I believe one has to know what spiritual enlightenment is, even if one does not have any intentions to realize such greatness. Absoluteness makes us understand the total meaning and existence of life, helping in reducing our dependence on duality.

The *Gita* says that God himself is the creation; He exists within all of us. I cannot say whether this is correct or not. I believe it is for each individual to form his own opinion. According to the *Gita,* God manifests at two levels of *Brahman* (intelligence-energy); they flow in either absolute or relative aspects. The absolute is non-dual while the relative comprises of duality. Therefore, we have awareness as the subject in absolute, and consciousness being a part of it, as objective in its relative aspect. We are a part of that absolute Creator in content, but as we exist in dualities, we need to shepherd the separated energy back into its oneness in order to realize pure consciousness in the form of God.

Many Western philosophers and intellectuals have visited India to study this aspect of life, a philosophy on duality and awareness over five thousand years old. Some have gone back dejected while others have written books on which the basis of spiritualism rests today, merging the two aspects for the benefit of humanity.

Hinduism has always been more of a philosophy than a religion. It is a way of living, where people from any caste, creed or religion are welcomed and embraced. This can be seen and evidenced in a small hillside town in North India called Rishikesh, which is the birthplace of spiritualism. Thousands of people come to Rishikesh from all over the world, mainly to understand the depths of yoga and spiritualism. There is no conversion in Hinduism, but sheer oneness exists.

In response to an article in a spiritual portal called 'The Speaking Tree', I had put forward a comment on Hinduism which is as given below:

'Hinduism is first a philosophy, a 'way of life' more than a religion. When esoteric people, take advantage of local rituals and culture from the heritage of any environment, religion takes birth.

In Theism, there is always a belief on deities (a person or thing revered as a god or goddess as the Supreme) Hindus believe in Paramatma or Supreme Energy. It has no beginning or end; it cannot be created nor destroyed. The Creator is the creation Himself. "Tat Tvam Asi" or I am That. It is when the form becomes formless in total awareness through pure consciousness, realizes the status of paramatma in pure energy.

As per Wikipedia "Nir-isvara-vada" statement of no lord or the doctrine of godlessness or disbelief in God or gods has been a historically propounded viewpoint in many streams of Hindu philosophies.

Hinduism is first a philosophy than a religion. The divine is present in all, rejecting a personal God, creator God, or a God with attributes. They may share the same cultural and moral values, which we postulate as Hindu religion.'

If you take the state of Hinduism, today, as a religion, it is rusting like any other, weighed down by caste, creed, superstition, money, and politics.

Hinduism postulates two distinct aspects of the meaning and existence of life. The first aspect deals with the absolute form of existence and the second in dualities. In the first aspect, life is non-dual, there is no 'you and me', no body and mind and no religion or God. There is only oneness, where you live in selfless service and total awareness, beyond body and mind, as a part of that oneness, in totality, pure consciousness and bliss.

What exists in this Universe is nothing but pure and total energy called *Brahman,* an all-encompassing energy, which in itself is eternal and forever flowing. It has no beginning or end, it is in continuum, and when this energy manifests in the mind, it evolves into the intelligence-energy referred to as spiritual awareness. This energy is termed as gross, in the form of an object or matter, subtle in the form of the mind, and core energy when in the form of the real inner self called *Atman* or the soul.

This intelligence-energy comprises the whole of the Universe and can neither be created nor destroyed. There is no creator of the Universe; God is the creation Himself, present in all of us as absolute awareness. On manifesting in the human mind, this intelligence-energy becomes both subjective and objective.

You come from nothing and go back into nothing – a nothingness referred to as *shunya* or zero, which is also infinite, constituting everything in it. In this state, you are God yourself. You become immortal, living in non-duality and all actions are taken selflessly, in service to the Universe. When the Observer (absolute, as the subject of life) becomes the observed (body, as the object of existence), observing (the mind as the intermediary) disappears.

It can also be inferred that individual thoughts and emotions have no meaning; they are simply a part of the all-pervasive energy – the Absolute. This approach to life is called *Karma Yoga* in the *Gita*. There is no destiny operating in this philosophy, as one is not living for one's body and mind, but selflessly, only for service, as Jesus Christ, the Buddha and a few others have done.

Living a human life, in absolute consciousness, is referred to as an *avatar* in Hindu philosophy. An avatar does not live in mind-body consciousness, but is a reincarnation of divine energy, in total awareness, and is devoted to service for all in selfless love. Life, in such a case, exists at its highest level of consciousness, thereby bringing in a new awakening and enlightenment, achieving God-realization. Ram, Krishna, Jesus Christ, Zarathustra, Gautama Buddha, and Muhammad can be considered as *avatars* who have become infinite in their existence and traversed the path of divine consciousness.

The second aspect of life propounded by Hinduism is that of living in dualities. This way of life is one adopted by nearly all of us, where we live mainly within the object of our own body and mind, within limitations. We form religions and God is given a name. We allocate heaven to those who do good deeds; others are considered as bad and are consigned to hell. Here, reality is perceived through the prism of the knowledge gained.

Since God is relative in this aspect, we have the Devil or Satan inevitably appearing on the other end. One may have as many separate gods as one feels like; you may choose to pray to whom you like. In this aspect, destiny plays a big role; you live in fear and insecurity, even if you possess everything, you keep praying to your personal god (mostly in fear), to bestow luck and good fortune upon you.

The role of destiny is peculiar in our lives, similar to our belief in God. In dual existence, destiny is definitely present, which is why one person is born rich and another poor; otherwise we would all have similar lives, without any differentiation. You may be destined for anything with respect to your past actions. Those past actions may have created your present, but the actions in the now, which is entirely in your hands, are creating your destiny and your future.

The mind is like a double-edged weapon, with intellect and awareness making it so powerful that one can alter or even create destiny if one is determined to do so. Those who are strong and free in their minds, create their destiny. Especially when you are young, you do not heed either destiny or God, neither are you victimized by the mere notion that we are destined to do this or that. You change the course of your destiny by sheer grit, discipline, intellect and awareness. On the other hand, those who are weak, give in to destiny. They use destiny as an excuse, to justify their egos, thinking: *We are above average, but destiny never wished it so*.

The idea of the Absolute is definitely not for everyone and most of us have no intention of transcending body and mind into eternity. It is only one individual in a thousand years or more who gives up his/her life for the sake of humanity and reaches pure consciousness. However, understanding both concepts helps us in knowing what lies at the other end of our existence of dualities.

For this reason, I keep emphasizing that we need to inculcate as much awareness as possible in our lives, either through natural impulse or by discipline, in observance, watchfulness, or alertness. Awareness may provide that foresight which reaches beyond right or wrong, making us strong and free. Further, our thoughts in dualities are never neutral; they are always biased because of the choices made by our minds, hearts and emotions, with ego showing the way. Consciousness exists in duality, until it becomes Pure or Absolute or singular. But awareness always remains singular, signifying who we really are, existing as the Witnessing Self within, the reason for us to be referred to as, "I am That." Awareness remains absolute and has no attachments or any bindings. One may find one's lover beautiful. Others may not, but in awareness, this beauty will shine out in its own true perspective.

We need to realize that 'I' am a part of the whole, and aware only up to that aspect of which 'I' am conscious (i.e. limited to my feelings, desires, sensations and attachments). These are the contents of my consciousness as of now. I am also aware that I am more than just body, mind and ego. Meaning, I am not just an object, but also the subject.

Total awareness is the Absolute, which is limitless, beyond time and space and non-dual. We are all a part of the Absolute, which is eternal and forever flowing.

Our reality too lies in this oneness; it is not possible for us to exist alone, we need to live with others. We have to co-exist in inter-reality. This way, everything and everyone, exists in connection to something else. Heat can only be defined in relation to cold, black to white; only then are we able to connect and maintain the cycle of life, in continuum and oneness. If there is higher separation of this energy, there is a proportionately intense surge in anxiety and despair. As dualities come nearer to their centre point, the conflicts in mind and body melt away.

Similarly, forms or objects are not divided into many. It's only our eyes that see them as separate. The fact that they are one is invisible to our eyes, because of our limited perceptions. All are connected as one continuous, formless wave of energy. Just imagine the state of sheer awareness of this inter-reality, inter-dependence, and inter-connectivity — it makes us so humble! This is what the Absolute is all about – oneness beyond our perceptions of demarcation.

With awareness, you begin seeing beyond, experiencing that life is unlimited — there is no beginning or end. It is only frequencies and wavelengths that our sense of perception figures is discrete in limited forms or objects. Like the sky, your eyes can focus only on a part, but in reality, it is unlimited. It cannot be measured or quantified, being timeless and space-less.

This oneness is the true self, referred to as the Absolute. Where body and mind form the outer being, coming from nothing and perishing into nothing, the inner being, the *Brahman,* is eternal, it is the supreme self. This Self is at the centre of all things called *Atman* or soul.

It is the same in all of us, comprised of that all-pervasive energy-intelligence. In human form, this energy is partly manifested as consciousness. In total awareness, the intelligence part of this energy liberates consciousness from ignorance, to the ultimate freedom called *'Moksha'*, where you travel beyond body and mind into absolute bliss, defined as God.

I repeat, in this concept of the Absolute, Self or *Brahman*, there is no dual or opposite, there is only acceptance and singularity. You do not live for the body-mind relationship. God and the Devil play a role only in the un-manifested intelligence of energy, by way of objective awareness. We are to rise from this ignorance and liberate our consciousness to travel towards the Absolute. In the same way there is no positive or negative. Both are the same — they are merely separated forms of the same energy, but you perceive and think of them as different.

In *Brahman*, there is no such thing as nothing; a glass is empty and full at the same time, either with liquid, solid or air, because of the continuum of its energy. It is defined as *neti, neti, neti* – neither this nor that: such is the nature of *Brahman*. Brahman, as explained earlier, is the Universe, which is comprised of one spirit. This spirit manifests as gross, subtle and core matter. It permeates, pervades, and prevails all that is. Scientifically, most of what exists in our Universe is dark energy and ordinary matter comprises only 4.9% of the Universe. According to Einstein, our Universe is also an optical illusion, for both matter and energy are interchangeable.

In the same way, Hindus introduced the integer zero in mathematics to the world, because zero too means 'neither this nor that', it is neither positive nor negative, yet it is everything. By itself, it is neutral, but when combined with any other integer, it quantifies positive or negative. Scientists realized that the ancient Eastern concept of 'nothingness' has a net energy of zero, meaning when we divide anything by zero we get infinity and also when something is divided by infinity we get zero. Always remember, nothing is everything and vice versa, and even if we are made of atoms, the inside of an atom is mostly empty space. Therefore, the source of everything is nothing, but the same is also within us.

In the Absolute, where there is no duality, even male and female are not considered to be opposites, but are taken as one. They are opposites only when they are designated as separate by the mind. They become one when they conjoin, to evolve further into this absolute or completeness. In ancient India, sex and spiritual living was very much akin to each other.

Sex was natural and meditative. It is during sex that all other thoughts were obliterated and orgasm was treated as the peak of meditation. It is also through sex that our dual bodies, being that of a male and female, conjoin as one, in total awareness. That is probably the reason we see various sexual postures sculpted on the walls of hundreds of ancient temples all over India. It was to go beyond physical lust and enter into the meditative field of oneness in awareness.

Khajuraho is one such marvellous temple, known all over the world. No modern religion can imagine such a mind-set as their attitude divides sex and the body into two. Even Hindus today, so segregated in caste, creed and modernism, fail to appreciate and understand this doctrine in depth, and carry immense guilt. Sex is no longer an open, natural subject, and brings with it a lot of misery in the form of lust, jealousy, and possessiveness.

To sum up, the Ultimate Reality or the Absolute in existence, as given by this philosophy, categorically states:

(a.) The soul, or source of the infinite spirit, the core energy, is present either manifested or un-manifested; it is the sum total of the existence of all that is, was or shall be.

(b.) The one in which non-dual intelligence-energy exists as pure consciousness is the absolute form of existence; when existing as un-manifested energy it is in its relative form, and because of its property of duality, remains an illusion, until complete.

It is only when you go beyond existence;
You become the source of that creation.

Chapter 12
Creation and Destruction

Creation and destruction are again two sides of the same coin. When we create something, we are automatically destroying something that existed before. This is because as per the Law of Conservation of Energy, mass and energy remain constant; it can only be arranged or rearranged in space in different forms. Science further declares that matter is pure energy in slow vibration, so matter and energy can neither be created nor destroyed: they simply change form.

This is what spiritual philosophy has been saying for over five thousand years, that we are all one consciousness, as intelligence-energy in one continuum. We are beings comprised of this energy, only giving the illusion of solidity. In ignorance, or as long as this energy does not revert to total awareness, we remain in dualities. We interpret the world through the perceptual thoughts of our minds, remaining wanderers between good and bad, etc.

The mind with its power to choose and discriminate separates this energy into perceptual thoughts. As long as we remain at the level of thinking, we exist in a state of dichotomies and dualities. Similarly, it has also been observed that the nature and flow of this energy favours a cyclic path rather than a straight one. From history to fashion to seasons, everything repeats itself in a cyclic pattern. Galaxies, stars and planets including the Earth, have been moving in circles around each other for billions of years.

Even in the solar system, we see cyclic patterns of planets orbiting the Sun, probably to maintain stability. From photosynthesis in plants, to subatomic particles in the microscopic world, these are all revolving in cycles, subject to a system and pattern of energy.

When everything, from the material world to all the systems of life move in a cyclic pattern, why is this not possible in the case of birth and death? If consciousness can bring life into matter and if as per quantum physics, energy is neither created nor destroyed, what stops us from believing that energy in the form of consciousness reincarnates, entering a new embryonic body to kickstart the heart and the mind into functioning?

This is probably how every creation in the Universe is stabilized and protected by the law of cycles; nothing is created nor destroyed, but keeps repeating in cycles of birth and death. Life continues, with birth and death simply functioning as entry and exit points for reincarnation. Awareness, intelligence energy, the core energy or soul, likewise shift in its frequency from one body into another.

Awareness, in such a case, is tuned into the frequency of its new creation, and so we face a new reality, according to the changed perceptions of a new someone. Life is a cycle of birth and death. The gross body and mind decompose and return to the dust from where it came. However, the intelligence-energy as the Soul/Witnessing Self transmigrates into another human being, to continue the cycle. This is how your body may die, but your individuality remains, strung together like beads upon a necklace forming One Unified Field of Consciousness. Your deeds are always remembered as who, what and when you existed upon this earth to fulfil your completeness in life.

In the evolution of birth and death, we have intelligence-energy, changing the raw mind into a conscious mind through awareness, forming a cycle again. We notice that the degree differs in each person, depending on each individual's capacity to transform and manifest awareness. The cycle remains intact, but a new relationship of mind, body and soul begins. It is important to remember that in the cycle of birth and death, energy, which cannot be destroyed, remains intact; however, it may change in its vibrations and frequencies.

Death is only a perception of the mind; we do not die in reality, as our spiritual energy continues. The intelligence-energy of our mind, our consciousness, is not destroyed. It may leave our mind, but it continues in its limited manifestation, seeking completion, probably entering a new mind in the hope of reviving itself better this time, until it reaches the final destination – ultimately finding that someone who realizes pure consciousness or the stage of enlightenment.

If this was not so, each new born would be identical in its intelligence-energy, they would behave like robots, in the same manner. What we see, however, are traces of past life characteristics, bearing the stamp of previous consciousness in each individual and then moving on, changing its reflections to continue and manifest fresh awareness into a new life.

We may argue that perception is what makes our world, without which only dark energy would exist. Even the Ultimate Reality or the Witnessing Self can exist only in the light of our inner perceptions.

Therefore, if someone were to ask me about the afterlife, my answer would be that on one end my inborn faith wishes me to believe in the same. However, on another, my logic tells me that a life worth living and thinking about is only in the now, which we tend to ignore and abuse. Therefore, have faith in yourself and live for the now in neutrality and humble acceptance.

When you are emotional,
your actions are impractical and prejudiced.
When you are spontaneous,
your actions are intuitive and imaginative.

Chapter 13

Spontaneity of the Now

The spirit in its true essence is defined by its presence in the now. The awakening begins when you recognize what truly exists is only the now. The past is gone and the future is yet to exist. Now is always there and will be, but the strange thing is that the mind finds it difficult to be in the now. Where lies the differentiation between the mind and the spirit? It is only when all three — past, present and future interconnect, that is, when we exist in the now while still connected to the past and future, we are complete.

Time and thoughts both relate to the past and the future, and hence are an illusion. Time cannot stand still nor can thoughts and that is why meditation is given so much importance; it teaches the mind to become still. Thoughts connect to past knowledge through which you plan your future. Between the reception of data and its transmission or reproduction by the mind, there is a loss of time, between the input and the output. This loss reflects in the mind, with the absence of the presence of the experiencer – in not being alive to the radiance of the present moment. It is because thoughts take time to produce that the mind loses the essence of the now.

In this manner, thoughts relate to whatever has already happened — relating to the content, which in turn connects to the body, senses, mind, memory, emotions, family, etc. This sort of identification is based upon a false identification of the self by the mind, forming a 'self-consciousness' termed: ego.

Ego, in its assertion of 'me and mine' believes itself to be separate from all others, glorifying its own existence directly or otherwise. It is necessary to de-programme people of the generations of layering in ego. This is primarily why spirituality requires 'knowingness', compassion, selflessness, awareness and a supreme effort to undo self-interest and the perspective of separation, distinct to the ego.

Every morning, the moment you awaken from your sleep, thoughts take over, reminding you of all that has happened and prompting you of what may happen. In this manner, your physical self is literally identified and controlled by your thinking mind. Your presence in thoughts takes place only in the past and nowhere near the now. This happens by your not realizing you are not the mind, because your presence is that awareness which can only exist in the now.

As long as the mind exists, thinking cannot stop, as the mind is purely designed to think and act. You see, smell, hear, touch and taste what your thoughts desire, giving rise to all your opinions, judgments, etc. This kind of mental structure sums up to merely 'remaining' — the collective conditioning of the past.

Spiritualism asks: is this what you really are? A product of the past reflecting that fact onto your future? It claims that when your chattering thoughts become aware enough to witness the same, you start the journey of living in a state of consciousness. When your mind is aware to be conscious of your presence in any situation, you are spiritually awakened. You are required to access that energy field prior to the onset of thoughts, to defeat the zone of energy, which has been conquered by ego in desire. Only awareness prevails in the now, prior to everything and is spontaneous. It can make consciousness move from content to context, because thoughts in ego will not let it do so.

Now, it may be simple to understand the concept of the now or living in the present, but how do you manage to actually do so? Especially when the mind is not accustomed to it? It takes time to convert and transfer the raw inputs from the sensory organs to the mind, and to decipher those into thoughts; in that moment, a new now takes the place of the old. There is a subtle deflection with thoughts, experience and intellect all playing their roles. The present moment exists in the presence of your awareness in the absence of thoughts, at that very moment. So, how do you capture that?

The only way you can experience the now is in spontaneity, before your thoughts emerge. The practice of simply being in the now is in itself a spiritual activity, which is to be performed by an individual who experiences total freedom in every moment of life. Actions taken with free will, rather than dictated by an external force makes a person spontaneous and natural.

The essence of awareness is in impulsiveness rather than residing in analysis by your thoughts. When you are spontaneous, there is a burst of fresh energy — the mind becomes intuitive, creative and imaginative. It is proactive and is free from calculative or emotional thoughts.

As explained earlier, when intelligence-energy is utilized by thought, it has a tendency to become contaminated with the old exhausted intelligence of the past. Thought is merely the conceptual representation of the 'I,' in the formation of ego. The ego, in turn, wants to possess everything in the body and mind. Aside from accruing wealth, fame and comforts for us, it mires us in a vicious cycle of pleasure and pain, anxiety, fear and depression.

When there is no thought, there is no 'I'. In the same way that we switch on a light and darkness disappears with brightness taking over, similarly, awareness penetrates the mind through spontaneity, and thoughts disappear. This is the basic concept of the Absolute. When awareness arises in totality, the body-mind complex has no further role to play. This invisible force keeps your soul alive in eternity. There is no role for the 'I' to reason, feel or derive logical facts, for these are mutable and limited to a specific space and time.

Therefore, in the first scenario, where all mortal creatures live with our small 'I', awareness is experienced only through flashes of creative intuition. Whenever there is a gap or stillness between our thoughts, awareness creeps in. This is the moment we get a chance to illuminate and expand our knowledge in spontaneity. Since these gaps are short and few, we need to practice discipline to escape the constant susurrus of our thoughts. Through impulsive observation or by the natural stillness of our subconscious, we can enlighten ourselves in spontaneous awareness. The art of stilling the mind is the practice of meditation. Mindfulness, in fact, is the art of increasing this gap between the thoughts. This happens when your mind is silent, but alert and watchful, in order to transform in awareness, from one moment to the next.

The ego confuses us; it keeps promising us better things and better times tomorrow, especially when faced with failures and errors. Ego gives us hope all the time, but this tomorrow never comes. You keep hoping for it, remaining unaware, bereft of enlightenment. In spontaneous awareness, it happens right there and then, in the now; it flows with subtlety, enlightening you and transforming you into something fresh and new.

I have heard and read this phrase many times, that 'you are what you think' and that you can achieve anything in the world by thinking. It is said, that if you desire a Rolls Royce, if you do not think about it, how are you going to get it? In my opinion, the mind has the capacity for drawing in additional energy from beyond our mere thinking processes. This energy plays an important role in our achieving extraordinary results.

If the mind had only thoughts to rely on, then all of us by sheer demand and thinking would have obtained everything we needed. The principle of 'think and it shall be given', is based on 'The Law of Attraction', on the presumption that to think is to ask and that your thought automatically finds a way to manifest your desires. If it was that simple, then imagine in a race, if there are two competitors who are ahead of others, but running neck-and-neck and both are thinking of winning, how is it that only one does win?

Suppose you are sitting alone by yourself and turn on some music. You become so absorbed, that your mind gets lost in that melody and you start dancing, forgetting everything in the rhythm of that music, and losing all sense of time and space. Abruptly, a thought appears and disturbs this beautiful rhythm; then more thoughts appear on other subjects, and now your connection with what you were listening to or dancing to, is just not the same. Hasn't that happened to you?

Likewise, your mind is accustomed to thinking about so many things at the same time, that by only relying on thoughts and intellect to play their role, our minds remain in the average and mundane realm, lacking imagination. Some magic is required, for phenomenal results. Something beyond thought and intellect, which we can capture if we really desire to obtain something spectacular.

Thoughts brood on the past and future; they are biased and emotional, limiting concentration and creation. Where every move is a reaction to a stimulus, there is no freshness. If you ask those who have reached great heights, they will tell you that the best phase of their progress came about when they were in action rather than in thought.

Imagine if a painter, designer, or scientist, keeps thinking of how much he is going to accrue in fame and money from his work while working on a project. Isn't he bound to adulterate his creativity? This is what I mean by saying that thoughts are an obstruction to creativity. Further, thoughts have a tendency to flow in multiples, instead of being focused on one subject at any given moment. They keep going into the past or the future. Then what is it that makes you achieve your dreams in life?

A strong receptor is embedded in the hard disk of your brain, the subconscious, which knows what you wish for. There is no need for you to keep thinking about the same thing. You need to get up and act, and bring in fresh energy through immediate awareness. You may remind your subconscious of your aims – say, by pasting pictorial representations all over, so that it keeps alerting your mind, but not by brooding.

Thinking makes you react, it slows you down, whereas in action there is no time for thinking; your mind functions on pure new energy in a higher capacity. In this mode of functioning, the subconscious directs your mind and body on autopilot to perceive what it desires, and then acts. The higher the intensity of the desire, the more the passion and the more the subconscious is activated towards this field. So the question is, are you then able to achieve what you really want?

Yes, but only for a select few, because our thoughts are so overpowering, that most of us remain victims of our thoughts and only keep dreaming. Those who are alert, astute, disciplined, clear, focused, observant and aware, they have moved away from their thoughts, have a better chance of achieving what they want. This is the way they build their own personal power, which drives their thoughts not in the direction of their emotions, but towards what the intrinsic awareness within commands. Either these traits occur naturally through the subconscious or they need to be inculcated, so thoughts are disciplined to remain quiet.

Do whatever you do, eating fast food
to living with mobile phones.
However, always question the way in which you do it.
Pause, look, and reflect before doing.
There are many who would want
You to blindly follow what they do.

Chapter 14
Personal Power

What is personal power? It is the ability to control your thoughts, impressions and energy levels. It is living in a state of awareness, which is higher than what the sensory organs can absorb. It is what I would like to refer to as what you really are. It is the presence of you, in your personality or individuality. The degree and quality differ in each one of us, and you need to grow, strengthen and balance it through awareness, for your subconscious to be aligned with this special 'self-consciousness'.

Personal power is the psychological sum of emotional flow and supernatural energies in any individual. It is derived from the subconscious and is what we really are. It is our uniqueness. It gives us the strength to make hard choices, manage our emotions, and not allow outside forces to dictate our lives.

In such a state, thinking functions only as a medium. It is a combination of past awareness and extra energy; it comes in as a booster, to provide thrust. This extra energy differs in each one of us; it is personal power, which takes us to our destination. Those who inculcate strong personal power in themselves are never dependent on anyone. Those who have achieved success have done so not just by thinking, but also by converting this extra energy into action, to lead them to greater heights. This personal power makes us realize that God resides within us.

The reason the mind is underutilized is we are not proactive with our personal power. We react to our thoughts under the weight of our past and future. We use our minds mainly for condemning, justifying, judging, evaluating or just dreaming. The mind becomes alert only when thoughts are kept at bay and we embrace spontaneity by grabbing fresh intelligence-energy to fuel creativity. Then you are aware of what you want in totality, seeking with your eyes fully open and other senses alert. Here destiny or just merely wishing via thoughts has no relevance. You are totally in the now; commanded by your subconscious into that oneness, where the rhythm flows only between you the creator and the object in creation, from one moment to the next.

It is your awareness, which is always in the now, spontaneously ready to absorb the freshness that can propel you towards what you wish to achieve, bringing in that extra energy for you to rise faster. Genetically, some minds are submissive, not at all aggressive. With discipline and determination, even in such cases, inculcating an awareness of the present moment, can achieve wonders. If you wish to remain strong and successful, never surrender your personal power. Life is beautiful and you have to design and direct your body and mind in awareness and in the now, fully experience its dynamic beauty.

A conscious life should be such that there is awareness, where actions are taken in the spontaneity of the now, in unity with the programmed intellect of the subconscious, acting through the conditioned reflex, showing full intention and an attitude of cohesion in thinking, feeling, saying and doing towards that action. Both the subconscious and the conscious should be in oneness, in totality and godliness.

In this manner, constant awareness becomes a part of your subconscious. For instance, once you have learned a certain thing, it becomes an automatic response in your subconscious, and you need not learn the same again. By making constant, choiceless and instinctive awareness a habit, your subconscious is awakened and remains alert.

You may ask why awareness should necessarily be contingent upon the spontaneity of the now. It is simply because the mind is dependent on its past and future thoughts, which limit the mind. The mind is a machine that is designed to desire. It mainly knows how to pursue or brood. When it is in quest-mode, it is wonderful, it achieves, and you progress. The same mind can also become your enemy, especially when it broods. It then oscillates between the past and the future, disturbing your equilibrium. It agitates, disturbs, and makes you nervous and anxious.

In this manner, the mind, when filled with only perceptual thoughts, always tries to move into the future, relying on past data. The thoughts in your mind, as discussed earlier, cannot be in the present because when the mind is open to the now, or the present, thoughts freeze. It is like the needle of a watch, which cannot stay in the present; it either moves into the future or stops. The now, in fact, is strictly the domain of awareness, whether you listen to it or not. The fresh awareness of the now enables you to balance your biased thoughts. Imagine how kind nature has been to us, in showering such a gift upon us.

In the now, meaning from one moment to the next, you are what we refer to in spiritualism as being in a no-mind zone, which is devoid of thoughts. This no-mind is the essence that I wish to capture; it is where all awareness, meditation, spiritualism and truth exist. This is why we can never aspire to the truth, we can only feel or experience it. The truth is always in the present; thought captures truth, only when it has exercised itself. Meaning, the moment you pursue it, you are enmeshed in the thoughts of the past and you start to exist in duality.

If you go to a spiritual centre, seeking how to be desire-less and ego-less, even then you are pursuing something. If not worldly desires, maybe desire for inner peace. The truth is, you will keep pursuing things because the mind's mechanism is set up in such a way. You may think you have reached your destination, but your mind is still full of desire and will always remain in duality. You will oscillate from one to another and that means you still exist in both, turmoil and peace. So what is the answer to this riddle?

Do not try to decipher truth through what you see, hear, smell, taste and touch. External perceptions through sensory organs are apparent and not true, as they are subject to change depending on the direction given by your internal perception in the form of experiencing that truth, which will also differ from person to person. It is only awareness in the now, which will lead one to experience the truth in its reality. That which is changeless is true, like the sun and the ocean; whereas the rays of light and waves in an ocean come and go, remaining apparent.

Truth is reality and that is permanent and changeless. Love is truth. Both are an experience, which cannot be defined in words that will dilute its essence, flowing in thoughts, from one to another.

For this reason, spiritualism only relates to experiential living in the now as the truth and not in what you see and hear. Truth is 'what is' just as it is; it is not a propriety of anybody, but everything belongs to truth, reality and love, the absolute. In its dual form, it separates into its relativity in the form of lie. So let truth be as it is, just be.

As children, we are so spontaneous, without bothering, fearing or thinking of the results of our actions, enjoying today to its fullest. As we age, the situation changes. The now disappears; we become conditioned to living in the past and the future. The reason — we are not designed to be aware of 'now', in the manner that we are aware of time. Unlike animals that can think only of the now, humans can choose and discriminate between the past, present and future. Every thought and bit of knowledge gained connects to our past. Our 'now' sadly, is mostly spent on planning, brooding or worrying about the past or future, without even being aware of the fact.

This is because of the factor of time. Time never waits, it keeps moving. It becomes impossible to identify your thoughts with the now, because of the impermanence of time. This is why thoughts always connect to the past. Therefore, we are seldom aware of 'now', primarily because of our direct relationship with time, which is always moving, preventing us from experiencing the present. At the same time, being also means to exist and existence is always in the now. This is the source of all the problems in our lives, where instead of concentrating or meditating in the present, our thoughts are always mixed up with this and that in the past or future, corrupting our now.

The culprits are our cravings and desires, gnawing at us, from all directions, disturbing the present and our peace; never-ending, wanting something or the other. You never know when and how to put a stop to these urges, always related to the future, but with a connection to the past. Suppose there was no desire, then there would not be any need for choice, discrimination or even duality. We would all be perfect. The answer – reduce your 'thinkingness' by 'knowingness.'

Every human being, whether a preacher, leader, spiritual guru or ordinary person, lives with desires. It could be a desire to embrace God, money, love or fame. This is why the mind with its constant wants, lives for tomorrow, because desire connects to future wants.

In worldly life, thoughts are primary. It is basically through the thoughts from your ego that you analyse with emotions and are energized into taking action. In spiritual living, thoughts are merely an interpretation into words of something that has already taken place. Thoughts separate energy from their oneness to function in dualities. To counter this phenomenon we require awareness to form into a Witnessing Self within to ensure that our inner perception balances this outer perception.

Science claims that everything in this Universe is composed of nothing but energy, which is interchangeable with mass and remains constant. Quantum physics declares that energy is the all and everything of our Universe, whether it is in solid state or a stream of light, it exists in continuum. We all come from this energy and go back into it.

This definitely makes way for the proposition that aside from our finite, mortal mind and body, which is composed of matter, there is in us an infinite intelligence-energy, referred to as consciousness, which is formless and limitless. Awareness in the 'now' is infinite and is the very basis of time, but is also beyond the realm of time, beyond space, beyond anything that our mind can perceive and think of. It cannot be cut nor divided, being the subject of everything that comprises our Universe. Anything aside from this is finite and limited in space and time, becoming relative and dual in order to exist.

The moment we recognize our soul, in the form of core energy in total awareness, we reach that stage, which is, referred to as absolute existence. It takes us into the true and real centre of our existence. There is no duality there, no oscillation from past to future, no ifs or buts, no illusions of momentary happiness or sadness. There is just pure bliss in total awareness.

The answer lies not in having to start on this journey of absolute existence, but in being aware of our cravings and desires and keeping a check on them. Understanding awareness and the composition of absolute existence takes us closer to our real being, to be in the 'now' as much as possible. This is what is called, the absolute truth.

Awareness is the only power within us that can hold or stop us from drifting here and there or from the past to the future. We need to still the mind, move away from thoughts, to enter into that no-mind zone, where we can invite creativity to enter our beings through the spontaneity of the now, for that newness to be absorbed into our minds, in the space between our thoughts.

Sensitive awareness is sublime 'knowing' in understanding, appreciation, and compassion.

Chapter 15
Sensitivity versus Sentimentality

Sensitivity is the intensity of our emotional reaction to other people. Normally, most of us are sensitive only in the areas where our personal relationships or self-interests are concerned, making us indifferent to what is around us. In such cases, whenever there is an exuberance of emotions, it is mainly directed towards a select few. This actually means we are sentimental, rather than sensitive. Sensitivity should be towards everyone, just like biologically you are sensitive, as you react to any stimulus.

Sensitivity demands a calm, serene and alert mind, where one can comprehend the feelings of others. It means not being only preoccupied with one's own self, but also to be responsive to others. It involves alertness and observation of what is happening around. The higher the sensitivity in any individual, the more the awareness of what is happening all around.

Just as lust is often mistaken for love, similarly, we confuse sentimentality with sensitivity. Awareness enhances sensitivity, leading to the evolution of a higher consciousness. In an unconscious state, one is unaware or is not interested in the whole, but attached or sentimental about only a select few. The mind remains obscured from reality and because of our limited attachments, we become sentimental.

To be sensitive, one needs to be responsive, aware, and willing to accept everything and everyone as is and change accordingly, from moment to moment. If you look inwards, you will notice that you have become so insensitive that your relationships with people are deteriorating, making you lonely. Today, there are more crowds, but we find ourselves alone. You may be more attached to your dog or cat at home, than your neighbour. This is probably because animals do not question, demand or argue, but simply give love.

The moment you attach, you become more sentimental and emotional. Your attitude becomes biased, your love is divided, and you become separated from its totality. In attachment, you become possessive; your love is a bargain, full of expectations, wanting a return for what is given. One day, such dual love is bound to bring grief and hurt. Remember, the degree of hurt is always directly proportional to the intensity of one's expectations.

As humans, we cut and divide everything for self-interest. This is the main cause of our sufferings. When you see anything in its totality, in its wholeness, know that it is real existence. The nearer we are towards the totality of any subject, the more centred and blissful we are. There is less agitation for this and that. Life is simple, humble and aware.

Alternatively, say, you have dedicated decades of devotion to your beloved, out of emotional attachment; if you do one thing wrong you could damage the relationship in a single day – a relationship that you have cherished for so long. This is how fragile attachments based on sentiments are.

The love that flows with zero expectations, asking for nothing in return, remains pure. Such love is referred to as 'absolute' and is the reason for saying 'Love is God.' To be sensitive, even love has to flow out in choice-less awareness, more from the mind, less from the heart.

Relationships do play a big role in our lives, especially those that are moving rather than stagnating. When family relationships tend to become more and more demanding, attachments increase, sentiments are aroused, duties and responsibilities increase and you start feeling a sort of burden. Your love starts stagnating, changing in kind and degree from its inception in purity and creativity. The way you are right now, the way you act and think, determines what type of relationships and love you have with others in your life.

Everyone says we love God, as He is not there to demand anything from you, and it is also convenient for you to love God, as and when it pleases you. Jesus said, "Love thy neighbour," and that is what is difficult. Here is a delicate relationship, which moves from one to another, creatively with sensitivity and choiceless awareness. Sensitivity should not be restricted to any one person. The environment sensitizes you by not allowing your mind to select and choose. This sort of relationship is refined and delicate; there is a movement of love from one to another, in awareness of the now, without any emotional or egoistic thoughts in self-interest.

Always be sensitive towards others. It is sensitivity that will make you aware that love is neither your property nor is it a tool for bargaining. Love is universal, eternal and free. In duality, love is fragmented and becomes related to hate. When love flows out of sensitivity, it feels for what is happening around and this itself is awareness, bringing in its wake generosity and detachment.

For matter to be alive, it needs motion.
For life to be alive, it needs existence.
For existence to be alive, it needs desires.
For desires to be alive, it needs a mind.
For the mind to be alive, it needs thoughts.
For thoughts to be alive, it needs awareness.

Chapter 16
Spiritual Living

Man has made tremendous progress in worldly life, but has left spiritual living far behind. The reason they clash is that they are opposite. One should pursue both in totality. Allow me to elaborate on how to balance between worldly and spiritual living in consonance. First, understand how each is required for existence, and how one can centralize life by practising both together.

When living in dualities, desire and self-interest play a dominant role in our lives. We permit the mind to become our master, becoming victims to our own thoughts, and forming our belief systems based on what our biased mind commands. In physical existence, dualities and opposites may be necessary but due to the never-ending feeling of want or desire, there is an inescapable feeling of incompleteness. The greater our comforts and materialism, the higher the insecurity; we cling to what we possess, making us feel insecure in always wanting more.

The reason is there will always be someone else who has more than we do, which makes us insecure; so the desire arises to prove that I can have more. Advances in science, technology, industrialization and agriculture, are only for our physical benefit, affecting us only on the periphery of our beings. Deep down we remain entangled in envy, greed, jealousy, and misery. We need to become wiser in order to observe and witness the games that our mind plays in ignorance. This is how we can awaken to realize the weakness behind the vicious cycle of pleasure and pain. This realization creates the need for cultivating a deeper knowledge of the self through spiritual living.

Spiritualism in no way denies anyone a good, comfortable, or wealthy life. In ancient Eastern texts, the four requisites for fulfilment in life are given as: righteousness, wealth, sensuous desires, and liberation. Worldly or materialistic existence keeps us centred only towards wealth and fulfilling desires. In order to experience completeness and totality, spirituality comes to the rescue, leading one first to attain wealth and desires in righteousness and finally to move onto the path of liberation. You will agree that righteous action should be the foundation of all that one seeks.

Many a rich or a powerful man is worried because his accumulations are not in accordance with righteousness, giving rise to anxiety and fear. There is no peace of mind in spite of wealth and riches. One's success, wealth and fame should be assessed only after knowing the means of attaining these riches, as the wealth acquired by the wrong means, eventually becomes a burden on the soul of that person.

Similarly, even in the case of desires, if you are prone to harming others to satiate your own feelings, they quite rightly, should be abandoned. If not, then they are bound to lead to further separation and grief. Righteousness or Dharma is crucial and should be taken into consideration prior to attaining wealth or fulfilling desires.

The sages were very sensible; they knew without worldly life of materialism that there couldn't be any liberation. After all, liberation from what? Therefore, economic progress and sensuous desires were necessary as an important part of education to awaken oneself from this ignorance of duality. But more important here is the righteous conduct, which precedes wealth and desire to achieve worldly comforts, as these are pre-requisites to go on to the path of the fourth and final stage of *Moksha,* liberation or salvation.

This is because the mind tends towards self-deception, self-bias and justifying its wrong deeds knowingly or unknowingly. One may adhere to laws and regulations under compulsion, but when it comes to morality or goodness, our divine energy is required to be consistently fair and loving towards all. Spiritual discipline and living guides you in that supreme vision in morality. Normal egoistic reasoning cannot go beyond self-interest.

Spiritual consciousness and realization lead us towards that direction where morality becomes a part of our existence. We will restrict ourselves mainly to morality in this discussion, since *Moksha* is not meant for everyone. *Moksha* is freedom, liberation or release from the cycle of death and rebirth, to become the Absolute in dissolving your body and mind in pure consciousness – an extreme and rare realization.

What is spiritual living? Firstly, it is not a theory that one acquires, from any master or even an institution. It is living in the now with spontaneity, observance, alertness, watchfulness and in awareness of the Absolute. It needs to be practiced by the individual alone, throughout his life. One cannot share the awareness gained by someone else. The word spirit is used because spiritual living involves intense attention, beyond thoughts of external perception, meaning, apart from the normal activity of the mind.

If the mind is a dictator in physical living, awareness is the saviour in spiritual living.

Spiritual living also involves living in totality and oneness with everything. This transformation makes us aware that in duality we keep judging what is good or bad, right or wrong, whereas absolute living demands no such divisions. Good and bad need to be accepted and regarded neutrally as one complete whole. Both are treated with equal respect, creating a co-existence between the two in well-balanced completeness.

Spiritual living takes us away from our physical mind and thoughts, not through suppression, escape or control, but by becoming aware of how the mind creates separations in every aspect of life. By giving in to greed, attachment, emotions, and blind beliefs, we create a deep demarcation between mine and yours, where mine becomes good and yours bad. However, who are we to judge? The reality of the Absolute is that we all are a part of the same universal energy, as one complete whole, and the more we distance ourselves from this reality, the greater the disturbance in the balance.

In my opinion, spirituality starts when we open our eyes and perceive the futility of living in a state of desires. It commences when we require changes in our day-to-day life, in order to fill that space or emptiness, within material existence. It is to probe deeper into the mind to discover the sixth sense, the mystical spirit, understand the real meaning of life for the sake of completeness and oneness.

There are different ways in which people approach spirituality, mainly due to the confusion created by mixing religion with spirituality. Religion is primarily a specific set of fundamental beliefs and practices, generally agreed upon by a community or group. Spirituality, on the other hand, is an individual practice for developing a sense of totality within and with others. It goes beyond the sense of perception and ego to draw upon your conscious experiences and discover the meaning of life. It is a quest to understand what lies beyond desires in self-interest and find a sense of unity with all.

Remember, in spiritual living, we require inner awareness at every moment. The reason is, the greater the knowledge you gain from here and there, the more your thoughts chatter, enhancing your ego. Spiritual living clarifies, "No knowledge is complete unless experienced."

Spirituality is best experienced by living rather than studying this subject. Its basic aim is to convey that the spirit as the observer, should be free to witness and not become entangled in the ego-consciousness of the mind. It exemplifies existential and experiential living to realize what life has in store for us.

There are times, when in spite of being spiritually aware, you give in to your vices or materialistic habits. It is human to err. As long as you can witness all that you think and do, moment-to-moment, awareness creeps in, watchful of what you are doing. You are bound to accept and outgrow these aspects of your personality to transform in spiritual living.

A spiritually realized person, who is aware, need not cut, divide or analyse everything with facts and logic. Such a person will educate himself with awareness first, rather than any other medium. When you just know and accept reality, there is strength in your deliberations. You will not need thoughts or intellect to support you all the time. It is the awareness of oneness and completeness that will lead you to decide which journey you should embark upon: that of the sensuous mind or that of the spirit.

Further, however rich, influential or intellectual one may be, one needs to awaken to the absolute reality of spiritual living. We need to decide to what extent our hearts, minds and bodies wish to take up this journey. Only then will we get answers to our questions on anxiety, despair, misery, loneliness and grief.

You may think and feel that you are not a victim of such negativity, so there is no need for self-realization. However, if you are in the cycle of joy and sorrow, money and want, you are bound to become a victim of circumstances – that day is never too far. Therefore, neither should you neglect worldly living in your duties and responsibilities, nor should you separate spiritual life from daily life.

In fact, most of us, I notice, retain blind beliefs with our minds groomed and rigid, full of what religion, parents, teachers, and gurus have inculcated in us since childhood. We have a dual personality – one for projecting to others, claiming this and that, another, which we refuse to admit or recognize how vulnerable we are, to any vice, in our self-interest. This is why it is imperative for us to first be true to ourselves before embarking on the journey of spiritual living.

I am the subject; I am the presence,
for I am that being who is aware.
I am that limitless, non-dual awareness,
separated from its subject.
Forming an object, as body and mind.

Chapter 17
Completeness

The term 'completeness' used in this book has nothing to do with its dictionary meaning, which is: any object when all of its normal parts are present, is considered complete. Completeness in its specialized sense is one of the most important concepts of spiritualism and concerns the totality of our being. In completeness, the body-mind complex fuses with core energy, our soul, into that oneness where there is no duality. It is the meeting point of duality, where negative and positive become one.

It is the mystery of our existence, which science is just realizing, that we come from nothing, go back into nothing and that nothing is infinite energy flowing in infinite space, which can neither be created nor destroyed. This nothing is the spirit or energy, which is everything; this spirit is all that is and is all that we are – eternal and infinite. Body and mind are composed from and decompose into this nothing called energy.

Completeness signifies the pure presence of the Absolute, the all-existing energy, *Brahman*. It cannot be subjected to comparison in degrees, as it is not relative to anything. It is free of all bondage. It is emptiness; it is the limitless awareness in which everything exists. It is beyond mind and knowledge; it is pure nothing and the total awareness of who you really are.

It is that stillness, that quietness, serene and tranquil, in which anything can happen in any way, but where the totality and oneness remains. Completeness is the end of desire, want or interest in anything. It is in such completeness that we all exist, with everything inherent in us, yet not finished. Like a seed, complete on its own, but yet to evolve and grow into a tree to flower, its fruits turning into a seed again. We keep evolving and recreating to become better or worse, in separation from that complete self, for that is the nature of our duality. This continues until we revive this energy back into its final realization of completeness, which is referred to as the Ultimate, Absolute or God.

The Upanishads further mention that *Brahman*, the all-pervading intelligence-energy, is also *poorna*, or complete, which comprises the whole Universe. It is pure and complete in itself. This universal energy manifests in the mind in the form of awareness, from which the mind becomes conscious to think and experience, in order to develop its Self-consciousness. When combined with objects, Self-consciousness separates this energy into duality and ego, thereby enjoying varieties of existence in life. Until such time as the mind becomes fully aware through the various cycles of birth and death, to revive that separateness back into its oneness within the grid of Unified Consciousness.

When our mind is empty and in total awareness, and there are no thoughts, this is when we are absolutely complete – a true contradiction by the standards of the world. This happens when we just know and act, that is, when we do not need to think and act. For it is in knowing that we are bound to the eternal world. Thinking, in fact, will take us elsewhere, mainly towards duality. Thinking should be nullified for us to evolve into completeness. This is what is meant, when zero is considered to be complete as a unit or entity, but can become anything, positive or negative, when it combines with any other integer while it is nothing on its own – a void or *shunya*.

The zero as nothing or empty, also forms a full circle, a complete whole. Everything in life starts from nothing; makes a full circle and then comes back to nothing. From energy to life and back into energy, though remaining constant and complete, as energy can neither be created nor destroyed. Evolving from nothing and going back into nothing, is this our story?

It is only when we are complete that we are in zero mode, a state of nothingness – *Brahman, shunya* or zero. It indicates an existence that is invisible and mysterious; no theory or language can fully answer this question, or explain this phenomenon, it only needs us to be self-realized.

Quantum physicists explain that when you break matter down into its smallest constituents, there is nothing but atoms in an empty space. In the same way, any object or form, when simplified, is just atoms, which are ultimately made of energy, and between two atoms, is infinite space. So, matter or form in reality is formless and empty. Even in a solid state, when an atom is broken down, we discover that 99.999999% is empty space. The Universe also constitutes a similar emptiness of space. We exist in this infinite space as energy; which can only be changed from one form into another and yet remains complete. Everything we know and see is an inseparable part of the Universe.

Therefore 'I' or my body and mind, are nothing but a bundle of desires and transitory thoughts, which make our 'my, me and mine'. Be aware, if you move into desire, let it be through knowing rather than thinking, without being overwhelmed, because knowing will bring in that required awareness. Awareness, on the other hand is that cosmic intelligence-energy, responsible for the quality of our thoughts, deeds and actions, in order to balance those never-ending desires.

Duality is un-manifested, separated energy, in that completeness; therefore, reality remains short-lived and transitory. As a cup on a table retains its identity only until it is broken, reality too may change into something else. Only the Absolute is changeless; you see or feel everything in total reality – it is seeing or feeling nothing.

In such oneness, there is no duality. Like the sky, which cannot be cut or divided, it remains one and complete in all respects. The Absolute is not for every individual; it is a state of dissolution, where there is no difference between creation and destruction. In this state, Buddha, Jesus or Krishna, just knew; they did not have to think to know. They were awareness themselves, fully manifested as the Absolute.

This is why in India we have God as both creator and destroyer, all in oneness. In fact, the destroyer is actually the liberator who frees us from the bondages of separation. For Him, all opposites have one meeting point, where good and bad, God or the Devil, life and death become the same – one. In this state of the Absolute, one does not need to think in opposites, one accepts both, in grace and peace, in total awareness. This is the philosophy of emptiness, zero or *shunya*. This is the only way ego and egoless meet at a point, where they become one and nothing – pure consciousness in bliss.

This book tries to capture and elaborate upon what has been explained through a philosophical treatise within a Hindu epic, which is thousands of years old – the *Bhagavad Gita,* which is a part of the *Mahabharata.* It is a text on the practical teachings of yoga. It also touches upon the basics of the science of consciousness, how to live moment to moment in daily life. As per Wikipedia, this epic has been highly praised by renowned scholars such as Aldous Huxley, Albert Einstein, Carl Jung, Hermann Hesse, Julius Robert Oppenheimer and many more.

According to the *Gita*, consciousness is a continuous flow of awareness. It is in the still mind, that awareness of the self reveals itself. Lord Krishna says, "You are the limitless awareness; the whole creation, as well as the lord, Himself is present." Awareness is the subject, the basis of everything; it is in this one and only all-pervasive awareness that all objects exist.

The main threat to humanity comes not from the Devil, as if there was some terrible mystifying force of ugliness, but our animal urges. It is our never-ending urges, our lust and desires, followed by outbursts of anger at any obstruction to our ravenous wants that lead to mental agitations.

What this book tries to convey repeatedly, is that if our intelligence is awake, we can consciously lift ourselves out of our sensuous selves. The reason being, the senses are superior to perception and the mind to the senses. Intellect controls the mind and what is superior to the intellect, is awareness – the *Brahman* (intelligence-energy) – present all around, forming the basis for the intellect.

This awareness is Him, within and without. The *Gita* revolves around the science of consciousness, telling us in detail about the methods required to develop one's personality. Not by following any religion or even spiritualism, but by oneself, day-by-day, moment-by-moment, in full awareness. The *Gita* shows us the path to a complete life.

Man eventually has to give up the notion of the limited 'I' of body and mind and replace it with knowledge of the limitless Self. In religion, promises of redemption are commonly made; stating that provided you do this or that, God will not grant forgiveness. According to the *Gita,* you are God yourself, full of existence, awareness and knowledge; you just need to awaken and arise to revive that godliness within you.

One's life should express, reflect and manifest

creation as far as possible, which is really, self-expression. Let awareness do the telling, for your mind limits concentration, especially when your thoughts keep running back and forth. Awareness will tell you much more than sensory perception, and this is what creativity is all about. What you need to do is to be true to yourself and act. Thoughts, when stimulated with awareness rather than feelings, is what the *Gita* refers to as meditation.

Life is like a seesaw, on one end we have relative or apparent reality and on another, the Absolute. Awareness is the pivot balancing the two. When we are centred in life, there is balance. If we are more engaged in the dualities of life, then we tilt towards ignorance and instability. If we become devoted to accepting everything in oneness and awareness, then there will be bliss centralizing both. Meaning, life has to be accepted, in its outer and inner spheres, as they are both a part of the same energy and are not opposed to each other. We need not choose one over another, going into extremes. All we need to do is remain in balance through awareness and lead a healthy and normal life.

In the here and now, accept and meditate, live from moment to moment and use this knowledge. That is what spirituality should be. Move subtly away from the chattering of the mind; bring in awareness of observance and acceptance, rather than brooding upon the past. In reality, in the now, there are no problems; when any event occurs, you are to accept and act, but when we look at reality through our thoughts, then yes, there seem to be problems.

To achieve the reality of absolute or pure consciousness, I agree, is very rare and not possible in materialistic life. Even then, the knowledge of knowing becomes necessary in our lives in order to be watchful, alert, observant and aware, to live every moment of life with clarity. Do not allow emotions or personal feelings to cloud your thoughts. Try to move towards absoluteness or completeness, knowing both the extremes, rather than residing in the illusions of dual life.

I cannot resist mentioning one of my favourite verses, giving the literal meaning of the *Shanti* Mantra from the Upanishads: "That is complete; this is complete. From that completeness comes this completeness. If we take away that completeness from this completeness, only completeness remains."

In duality, our spirit, even though complete because it is absolute in its content, remains unfinished due to the separation of this energy into opposites. Life, in its cycles of birth and death continues in its journey of experiencing and realizing, until it reaches the final stage, what we refer to as Self-realization, Pure Consciousness, Total Awareness, Absolute or God, where the completion is finished, when in totality, we become eternal in the form of the divine. Where there is no distinction or separation between body, mind and soul. It is all finished in totality as ONE, absolute ingredient.

This is a complex concept but equally interesting to know. We are not to take 'complete' to mean 'finished' or the end of the matter because in creation, there is nothing finished, everything is a progression, each cycle of life keeps growing and evolving from one form into another, but remaining constant in itself.

The same phenomenon, science explains, is in the Law of Conservation of Energy.

What it says is, we are complete in our own selves without being finished, as a seed is complete in its own, yet grows and flowers into many more seeds, in different variations. Intrinsically we have everything in completion within us, but also have the faculty or potential, to remake or revive a new self again and again, because nothing is ever finished. The body may die, but life continues, passing from one body to another, remaining constant.

Completeness therefore refers to the ever-complete absolute energy, which also exists in a vacuum. The total amount of mass and energy remains constant, you cannot add anything extra nor may you subtract anything from the total. Scientists know this completeness now as universal energy. In ancient days it was called *Brahman,* the Ultimate Reality.

How beautiful! Nothing is complete, yet completion remains; from that comes this completion, because everything we need in this body is already, inherently there. It is for us to self-realize and revive back into totality.

Awareness on its own is nothing.
Like zero on its own is nothing,
Both, on manifesting are everything.

Chapter 18
The Power of Zero

Have you ever wondered who invented the number zero? Can you imagine mathematics or science without the zero? The number or the word 'zero' makes our lives smooth and easy — in fact, we simply cannot function without it.

According to Wikipedia, Babylonians were the first people to use this symbol, but not as a true zero because it was not used independently or at the end of a number. The concept of zero as a number and not merely a symbol is attributed to India, where most of the numerical system first originated and practical calculations were carried out using the zero. Indian scholars used the Sanskrit word '*shunya*' to refer to zero, which means void, emptiness, or nothing.

What is mystifying about *shunya* is that when a number is raised to the power of zero, the result is one. Similarly, if we are raised to the power of *shunya* or nothingness, we become one – a unity or oneness. Let us delve into this mystery and learn how powerful this zero is, especially about the metaphysical realm. By itself, it may be nothing but when attached to something, it is everything.

Today, the zero serves as a placeholder, taking its place between or after numbers in our counting system. Zero comes in after nine to 'roll over' and is a definite number, so we cannot say that it is nothing. We may say it is neutral as it quantifies any numeral, positive or negative. For example, if we combine zero with -1, the number goes up to -10; similarly, +1 becomes +10 and so on. In metaphysics, too, we cannot define zero as nothing because the absence of something is still a thing, for instance, air in space or in the sky. Therefore, we can say that zero is a link or connectivity, which on its own may mean nothing but does correspond to something when connected.

Zero may mean emptiness; however, at the same time, it is in perfect balance between positive and negative, forming an equilibrium. Alternatively, it is infinite, as it has no beginning or end. It is neutral. It quantifies an integer when attached to it, whether positive or negative. The number zero is as alive as any other number because without it there would be no mathematics, algebra, or even science.

The zero is mysterious. As I mentioned, even the absence of something constitutes *something*. In eastern philosophy, this something, nothingness, or emptiness of *shunya* is considered a cosmic void. All existence emerges from *shunya,* coming out of nothing and dissolves back into nothing. In other words, it is the pure presence of everything, like the sky. The sky itself may be empty but it is the pure space where everything comes and goes – yet, the sky remains the same.

The state of *shunya* in Hindu philosophy, aside

from its numerical meaning, is also understood to be a state of all-pervasive *Brahman,* the Ultimate Reality that is always present in the Universe, which becomes alive or comes into existence only when it merges with the mind and body.

As per the Vedas, the sacred texts of the Hindus, within this *shunya* or zero lay the philosophy of existence. What we call 'zero or nothing' is in reality the source of everything. From this very *shunya,* referred to as absolute zero, manifests the whole Universe – it is called *Brahman,* where all-pervasive *Brahman* (awareness), the supreme energy, prevails. Both *Brahman* and *shunya* are similar, as both emerge from emptiness and are as nothing, until they manifest. One reveals its presence by joining with matter in becoming the mind and the other manifests by quantifying itself with other numerals.

Both *Brahman* and *shunya* are un-manifested energy, lying in the emptiness of nothing. A stand-alone zero is nothing; it manifests the moment it combines with other numerals. In the same way, *Brahman,* awareness or cosmic intelligence remains neutral on its own and manifests by flowing out of the cosmic emptiness, joining matter by entering the mind. Therefore, the state of *shunya* and the state of awareness (*Brahman*) are the same – nothing on their own but the sources of everything.

The quality of the mind or its intellect is dependent on the awareness manifested in it. Only then the mind, is said to be conscious, just as the zero is dependent until it combines with other integers. This is how we become different from other solid objects. It is the reason why God – who is omnipresent, omniscient, and omnipotent – is a synonym of awareness, present in every single cell of our body, allowing us to presume that we are God ourselves.

What is projected from the mind is nothing more or less, than what is projected by the Lord himself. Both come from the same awareness, meaning from the same origin or source. Therefore, I as body/mind/matter am zero and my ego is zero, being limited. However, when I merge with all-pervasive awareness, I rise in divinity and come nearer to the origin, to reach the level of the Lord himself.

Science has realized that everything is energy. The entire Universe is like a web, tied together by a common invisible energy in the form of different vibrations, frequencies, and wavelengths, which ultimately point to a single interconnectedness. We are all manifestations of the same energy. This energy or awareness is eternal and forever changing, relative, when we are in ego, consciousness and absolute, in purity. Virtual atomic waves and particles spontaneously appear out of empty space or *shunya* and exist before dissolving into empty space, and reappearing yet again.

In every aspect, physical reality is just a manifestation. We may see it in different forms, but it is a single universal energy that encompasses everything that we can imagine in all that exists – not in isolation but in a continuum. Just as a fish exists in an ocean, we exist in the sphere of energy, space or *shunya*. What appears solid is only so because of the way our senses are attuned to perceiving certain vibrations and frequencies.

We do not see or feel what our minds cannot perceive. We can only see disjointed parts of the energy of different objects, as solid forms through our limited perception. Therefore, the sense of a physical self is a perception of our limited minds. As Einstein explained – matter and energy are interchangeable; they are essentially one. When matter is broken down to its miniscule form, it is the same as energy.

Centuries ago, philosophers postulated that all physical existence was composed of five basic elements: earth, fire, water, air, and space. Science has reframed this concept: matter with energy, space with time, and intelligence or awareness with consciousness. Science views consciousness as the second level of awareness in experience, vaguely referring to the same as an epiphenomenon of electromechanical reactions, forever flowing through the topology of space.

How this intelligence-consciousness forms a common link with matter and energy has still not been confirmed. Neither have we been able to prove that human beings are connected to one supreme self, God, or a greater creative force. As of now, this remains a matter of belief. Eastern philosophy proclaims that matter (energy) has the quality of existence ('*sat*') and when one achieves the highest levels of consciousness ('*chit*') by merging oneself with absolute awareness or reality, by practicing yoga and meditation, one attains bliss ('*anand*').

This is equivalent to becoming the supreme self or creative force, for example, Jesus Christ, Lord Buddha, Lord Krishna, or the Prophet Muhammad. To provide further clarification, I have given below a detailed explanation of the facts I have gathered in my quest to solve this mystery.

We are aware that our body, thoughts, knowledge, and sensory organs all have their own limitations. We hear the frequencies that our ears can process – but we also know that a dog can hear higher frequencies than we can. Similarly, the eyes of a bat or viper function differently than human beings' eyes. Therefore, we have our limitations, along with different levels of consciousness within us. I, as body-mind complex, may have limited power and knowledge, but the power of *shunya,* as described below, goes beyond the mind into limitless energy.

Sages from ancient India measured time through the concept of '*kshana*'. This is not chronological or psychological time; it is 'individual' time. *Kshana* is the time between two thoughts, differing from person to person. This empty time between two thoughts, the space of nothingness or emptiness, was also referred to as *shunya*. In this space, you are in a 'no-mind zone' – being away from the thought processes of the mind; you are in union with the absolute energy or the cosmic void.

Kshana is that moment of presence, in which you are face-to-face with the cosmic intelligence, void, or *shunya*. Therefore, *shunya* can be presumed to be that idle intelligence-energy eternally flowing in the cosmos. When it merges with the mind, it manifests as awareness. It brings existence or life into force or reality, in the form and content called consciousness.

In our world of dualities and dichotomies, an average person's thoughts churn with no logical sequence. Thoughts are always dancing in our minds, from the past to the future and back again. We may be thinking of great ideas and concepts, and then we may jump over to fantasies or may chance upon what we could have done or recall what someone else did to us, so on and so forth. If we pen down all the thoughts we have even in a short while, the result will seem like a crazy person's diary! It is impossible to suppress thoughts – trying to do so only leads to more thoughts.

Try watching your thoughts as an observer, without getting involved, and see the difference. They will resemble clouds moving in the sky, having no involvement with us. Your mind will gradually slow down and your heart rate will fall, allowing you to enter the gateway of the no-mind zone. This stilling of the mind is called meditation; through this divine pleasure, you can reach towards ultimate awareness, which is far beyond the reach of the active mind.

Kshana is the space between your thoughts when you are truly aware of your real self. In the case of an average, active, dual-minded person who is enmeshed in the vicious cycle of pleasure and pain, with the mind being agitated or excited, the space or time between two thoughts is very small. In the case of an enlightened or aware person, however, thoughts are no longer a bothersome impediment. The person remains in a no-mind zone for longer and becomes a master of observing his or her own thoughts rather than getting involved – then, *kshana* is longer and more blissful.

Meditation takes you toward a longer *kshana,* into that emptiness where you become calm and peaceful, internally as well as externally, showing positive changes in your mind and body. Scientists are just discovering this mental state and acknowledging that meditation is the elixir of life. In this state, the body and mind do not determine the quality of what you are. You are in contact with your source, the eternal awareness; the basis of all creation referred to as God. This is what meditation is: to become a part of *shunya,* to know life beyond limitations and the sphere of the physical, to experience the source rather than the mere outer surface of life.

This cosmic void is the origin and source of creativity; it is said that not a single thought emanating from the mind can originate from this void. Thought is merely an expression of the mind explaining what it has already acquired, whereas creativity is a reflection of the supernatural, a spontaneous flash of intelligence originating from the no-mind zone to merge with the mind.

Therefore, the mind or 'I' with all its thoughts can neither create nor meditate, probably because the mind is meant to plan, analyse and calculate. This is why many important events take place in our lives unexpectedly. It is the empty mind, the pure experience of the cosmic void that is the most creative – not the result-oriented, thinking mind.

Deep meditation is a combination of contemplation, meditation, and *samadhi* (merging with your source) – the highest stage in meditation, in which a person experiences oneness with the Universe. This is the stage or bliss that sages in India practiced to achieve complete self-mastery. Scientific studies have demonstrated the effects of intense meditation on DNA and gene expression. The positive effect of meditation at the cellular level in the human body helps delay the process of aging by increasing telomerase activity.

Telomerase is an enzyme that repairs DNA. Every time a cell divides, its telomeres become shorter and once a cell runs out of telomeres, it cannot reproduce anymore and dies. Telomerase reverses this process and enhances longevity. A research team at the UC Davis Centre of Mind and Body concluded: "… purpose in life is influenced by meditative practice and directly affects both perceived control and negative emotionality, affecting telomerase activity directly as well as indirectly."

Research on dreams and sleep has shown that deep sleep is necessary for our well-being; it helps rejuvenate the body and mind by producing 4–7 Hz theta waves. These electromagnetic waves maintain the body's health by producing and replicating good DNA. In deep meditation too, the same alpha and theta waves are produced, acting in the same manner.

All this tells us how important it is to possess control over our senses, limit our desires and attachments, and contemplate our thought processes to attain that silence within, travelling beyond the mind into the emptiness of this pure energy.

Most scientists and doctors have some belief in a

higher power or some creative force that transcends science; however, they do not yet have a way to prove the physical reality of this concept. Alternatively, as we mature, we realize that life is like a large prison where we are the prisoners of our thoughts, actions, and deeds. The higher the level of goodness within us, the more we become selfless, accept all that comes our way, and realize that this world is an illusion, which we are to transcend.

Whenever I have completed a good deed, the reward has eventually reached me (even though it may not come from the same source), making me realize that you reap what you sow. One also realizes that positivity, giving, love, faith, truth, detachment, and fearlessness are all akin to godliness. You need to become aware of the saying, "God helps those who help themselves", which further signifies that God is within you.

When we peer into the atomic world, the whole Universe appears like a web, tied together invisibly, with rhythm, harmony, and symphony. There is beauty and infinite space, where all the planets, stars, solar systems, and galaxies dance in a unique cosmic order, despite moving at great speeds. Quantum physicists claim that the whole cosmos is inseparably interconnected as one field of force, in continuum as a unitary field of energy. The ancient Hindu Upanishads (philosophical texts) consider this as divine, and have long known it as *Brahman*; a Sanskrit word signifying the supreme Ultimate Reality that does not change with space or time.

The statement '*Brahman* rises above everything' implies that the soul is the innermost core of our beings, and consciousness is the highest truth of awareness (*Brahman*). The Self or soul is nothing but God, when we transcend our relative, illusory or dual life to reside in the absolute in total awareness. This means *Brahman* is not created from something, but is ever flowing and is created from the reality of its own being, by combining as matter, when in slow vibration. In Aristotelian terms, *Brahman* is both the material as well the efficient cause of creation.

Carl Sagan, an astronomer and cosmologist who played a leading role in the American space program at NASA, wrote extensively upon ancient Hindu cosmology, using a now-famous phrase: "the great cosmic lotus dream". He also referred to the bronze statues cast in the eleventh century in the Chola temple in India as: "The most elegant and sublime of these bronzes is a representation of the creation of the Universe at the beginning of each cosmic cycle – a motif known as the cosmic dance of Shiva."

To sum up, let us travel into the zone of the cosmic void called *shunya* through meditation and experience a taste of bliss. This will deeply change your mindset, allowing calmness, balance, and serenity to blossom. Aside from chronological and psychological time, we experience individual time, which is the space and time between two thoughts. We should try to delve into this space to realize the ultimate truth and reality of our existence.

Shunya or emptiness will let us glimpse our origins, which lie beyond our questioning minds and make us aware of where we come from and what we will finally dissolve into – the supreme concept described earlier in detail as absolute awareness, a void called *shunya* – zero.

Epilogue

I hope this book was able to provide an insight into existence and its purpose. I have gone to great lengths to probe our thought processes deeply, explaining how thoughts, aside from being everything to us, are also responsible for making us self-centred and how emotions disturb creativity. If thoughts are driven by emotional intelligence, then what we have in contrast is awareness. Awareness comes to our rescue to foster creative intelligence, which awakens us from the illusions of life.

Ancient Hindu philosophy, propounded around 1500 BC and codified during 600 BC, explains how God and Creation are one, comprising all matter, energy, space, time, and everything around and beyond our Universe, existing in total awareness and in peaceful coexistence. I have based my books on this teaching. For centuries, man was under the impression that he is separate from all other creations. Today, science too agrees that God did not create the Universe and that we all come from one source of energy.

Contemporary religion is being exploited to foster violence and hate. My purpose in writing this book was first, my intense passion for Spiritualism. The second was to share the idea that spirituality, science and the material world are essential to us and always will be. One cannot do without the other. This way, we can recognize and amalgamate the reality and truth in our lives and we come close to understanding the meaning of God and creation. We discover that even science through its various truths is coming closer to the Truth.

The ideas, opinions and observations that I offer are what seem to be required for all of us to reach that state of consciousness where we are able to grasp the meaning and purpose of life. For all this, you will agree that your own participation is essential; these books can only provide a path towards that goal. In addition, you may not always agree with my opinions, but these are personal, with no intentions whatsoever to hurt the sentiments of any person, group or institution.

These books intend to convey two messages: first, in spite of living in duality, we need to understand the concept non-duality. Second, that duality is only in the mind, the real requires unconditional love as its fuel, to reach its final goal and that itself is oneness, between man and the Universe.

We need to channelize our consciousness, where one feels for the Universe and not only for the individual. The heart has a tendency to be selective and feel only for itself. Therefore, you might agree about the title of this book, which is an effort to convey that to shower love for all, one needs to think from the heart and love from the mind.

Allow me to quote a few lines from my third book,

which I feel is highly relevant here: "*We try to connect our hearts with love through our minds, though the heart is a physical organ. When we use words trying to speak from our hearts in a poetic manner, we call them emotions, but they are only thoughts in motion. Emotions too, though related to the heart, originate and settle in the mind, demanding something or the other in return. Therefore, even though emotions are connected to the heart by disturbing the pulse and heart rate, they are present in the mind rather than the physical organ of the heart.*

Always remember: love is neither a property nor a characteristic of the mind or the heart. Love is God. It is that presence, being in the now, as an experience for us to become aware, always wanting to give and not to take. Love is Supreme energy."

Since God and religion are all in the mind, love should be the only religion, so we can truthfully say 'Love is God'. With such a quantum leap, the purpose of life is bound to leap from ambition to meaning to awareness.

Acknowledgements

I am indebted to the following people:

Friends and family members, who encouraged me at every step, indulging me during my lengthy monologues on the subject of Spirituality. Their invaluable critiques helped me tide over doubts and rough stages during the writing process;

My Editors, for improving form and content, and patiently re-reading drafts of the manuscript;

To my wife Komilla Kumar, thank you for your patience, love, support and inspiration.

To my children, Nadisha Gulati and Shreeya Kumar Bhola, who will always be my creative force.

Finally, I dedicate this in memory of my parents, my greatest inspiration, for making me who I am today.

Notes

Notes

Notes